The Magic

ACRONYMS, FORMULAS,
& IMPACTFUL STORIES

of Leadership

The Magic
ACRONYMS, FORMULAS, & IMPACTFUL STORIES
of Leadership

A Tribute to the Amazing
Dr. Rob Gilbert & the Success Hotline

FOREWORD AND ADDITIONAL INSPIRATIONS BY DR. ROB GILBERT

The Magic Acronyms, Formulas, and Impactful Stories of Leadership: A Tribute to the Amazing Dr. Rob Gilbert & the Success Hotline

For information about this title, contact the publisher:

Andrew Marotta
www.andrewmarotta.com
andrewmarottallc@gmail.com

ISBNs:
978-0-9990055-8-3 (softcover)
978-0-9990055-9-0 (eBook)

Printed in the United States of America

Cover and Interior design: 1106 Design
Cover Picture: Mike Peters

Dedication

This book is dedicated to the super-amazing and incredible Dr. Rob Gilbert. Dr. Rob's dedication to the daily Success Hotline and his commitment to helping others have been astonishing. To do something every day—*every day*—since January 1992, is really remarkable. I dedicate this book to my friend, mentor, mental-strength coach, and inspiration, Dr. Rob Gilbert, professor of Sport Psychology at Montclair State University. Dr. Rob: Thank you, thank you, thank you. You have helped me and thousands of others reach their goals, be more confident, get past problems, and more. You are a Jedi, a saint, a legend, and a true giving spirit. I hope I made you proud by writing this book and sharing your life's work. So many of us are truly indebted to you for your inspiration, motivation, and more.

Thank you!

Andrea Marotta

TABLE OF CONTENTS

The Magic
ACRONYMS, FORMULAS, & IMPACTFUL STORIES
of Leadership

A Tribute to the Amazing Dr. Rob Gilbert *& the Success Hotline*

FOREWORD

by Dr. Rob Gilbert

OCTOBER 1979

You can change your life by altering your thoughts.

It was my first semester as a professor at Montclair State College in New Jersey. One morning after class, a student asked if I knew who "Eric Butterworth" was. I told her that I had never heard of him. She very enthusiastically explained that he was a Unity minister from New York City, with a 15-minute radio show that was on every morning.

The next morning at 6:15, I tuned into Eric Butterworth. The very first words out of his mouth were, "You can change your life by altering your thoughts!"

I instantly liked him, and, from then on, I rarely missed his radio program. Why??? Because I learned a lot from him! He had great inspirational messages, filled with quotes and stories. To this day, I still quote Eric in my lectures.

JANUARY 1992

It's better to do a little a lot than a lot a little.

The spring semester was just about to begin. I was still listening to Eric *every single day.* Over the years, I had attended a great number of seminars and lectures. However, Eric's 15-minute radio programs benefited me more personally and professionally than all those high-priced seminars, workshops, and training programs combined!

This semester, I was teaching my graduate course in Applied Sport Psychology. I love this course, but the one thing that always bothered me about it was that the class met only once a week. And that was for two and a half hours.

Before I became a professor, I was a wrestling coach at Hopkins Academy in Hadley, Massachusetts. I would have my wrestlers work out five, six, and sometimes even seven days a week! And now, I taught my graduate students only once a week? This made no sense because "It's better to do a little a lot than a lot a little."

That's when I had a blinding flash of the obvious!!! Why couldn't I be to my students what Eric Butterworth was to me? Of course, I didn't have the resources to host a New York City radio show, but I did have an old-fashioned telephone answering machine!

And on January 22, 1992, Success Hotline was born!!!

I told my students that, every morning for the next 14 weeks, there would be a new three-minute message and that I hoped that they would call and listen.

The daily messages were intended only for my students. I'd planned on leaving messages only once a day for the 14-week semester. My plan was that, after those 98 messages, Success Hotline would be done forever.

However, much to my *great* surprise, by the end of the semester, I had so many messages from callers from all over the country that I decided not to stop.

I guess I wanted to be just like Eric Butterworth!

MARCH 2024

WOW!!!

I am proud to say that I have continued with Success Hotline, and I have never missed a day. I have done a message *every single day* without fail for more than 33 years.

One day when I was at school, I received a package. I noticed, from the return address, that it was from a long-time Success Hotline caller—Andrew Marotta. Inside the package was a t-shirt. There was a picture of me on the t-shirt. Under my picture were these words:

The Magic Acronyms, Formulas & Impactful Stories of Leadership: A Tribute to the Amazing Dr. Rob Gilbert and the Success Hotline

I called Andrew immediately and said, "I didn't know that you were in the t-shirt business!"

He laughed and said that he wasn't in the t-shirt business—he was in the book business! He explained that the t-shirt was advertising a book he was writing about me and my Success Hotline!

WOW!!!

For one of the few times in my life, I was totally speechless.

I've always considered it an honor to write a book. However, having someone write a book about me and my beloved Success Hotline was not on my bucket list. It was not even in my wildest dreams.

Thank you, Andrew Marotta, for one of the greatest honors of my life!!!

Rob Gilbert, Ph.D.
Montclair, New Jersey
May 2025

▪ ▪ ▪

INTRODUCTION

973-743-4690

"***Hey, Andrew—you'll love this.*** You gotta call the Success Hotline." A friend of mine said this many years ago.

"What is it?" I asked.

He continued, "It's Dr. Rob Gilbert, and he leaves a three-minute message about success. He does a new one each day."

Wow—that's cool, I thought, and gave it a try. I called for a couple of days and, right away, loved it. I loved the messages, I loved that they were just three minutes long, I loved his voice, and I loved the whole thing.

I started to notice that I was recalling the message at different points of the day when things happened or situations would arise. I found the messages floating in my memory and saying to myself, "Ahhhh, *that's* what he is talking about." It began to feel like the messages were just for me. I got a black-and-white marbled notebook and started to write down the messages. I started to use them with my staff at school and on the court as a men's Division I college basketball official. I could hardly wait for the next day, when I could call again and hear the next message. I was hooked, and I hope you will be, too.

Ten years later, with five books of my own, a professional speaking career, and more, I am eternally grateful to Dr. Rob and his work with the Success Hotline. He and the Hotline ***literally changed my life*** in just three minutes a day. As I sit here writing this book, I still shake my head at how it happened. He is magical, the Hotline amazing, and, as he has shared many times, it's the results, the successes, and the positive impact on others that matter most. Enjoy *The Magical Acronyms, Formulas, and Stories of Leadership*. The stories are authentic, the sayings are real, the formulas work, and so on.

▪ ▪ ▪

HOW-TO

Pick a page—any page—and just start. You can go in order, you can flip, and you can go backward. However you want to read the book, have at it. I did my best to group the magic acronyms, formulas, and impactful stories into categories, listed in the chapter titles. Use them, live them, and, as Dr. Rob has said many times: *Put them into action.*

Repeating of phrases. You will find many parts of the book where I or Dr. Rob uses the technique of repeating phrases. It acts as a mantra or type of meditation. The formal term for it is *anaphora*: the repetition of a word or phrase in consecutive clauses, sentences, or phrases. It's used to emphasize a particular word or phrase, create a rhythmic effect, and *make the message more impactful and memorable.* That was our goal, and it's actually the goal of the whole book—make a meaningful, memorable, and positive impact on you while you're celebrating Dr. Rob and his work along the way.

Like the tips in the book and want more? *You got it.* In addition to the daily phone message on the Hotline, (973) 743-4690, Dr. Rob has many (not all) of the messages on his podcast on iTunes. Search "Success Hotline by Ironclad," and you can find it in most places where podcasts are found.

I wish you the best on your journey, and if I can help you in any way, don't hesitate to reach out on Facebook or by email at andrewmarottallc@gmail.com.

BEFORE WE GET STARTED . . .

Every once in a while, Dr. Gilbert talks about "the formula." This formula is the basis for all the Success Hotline messages.

Before we get started, I present the formula:

A + ST + GOYA = R+ or R–

Here's how the formula works: When you believe in your ability (**A**), combine it with the correct strategy (**ST**), and take action (**G**et **O**ff **Y**our **A**natomy), you will get a result (**R**). You will *always* get a result. The question is whether it's going to be a good result (**R+**) or a bad result (**R-**). If you get a good result—keep on doing what you're doing. It's working! Keep on using the same strategy. But, if you get a bad result—make changes to the strategy you were using, or find another strategy. As they say in the world of tennis, "Never change a winning strategy. Always change a losing one."

For example, suppose you decide to go on a diet to lose weight. If the diet is working for you: Keep On Keeping On. But if the diet is not working for you, do not beat yourself up and blame yourself. That would be doubting your ability. Instead, try another diet or another strategy.

In the end, no diet works for everyone, but every diet works for someone, so you have to find the diet that works best for you.

■ ■ ■

CHAPTER 1

ATTITUDE

It is your attitude, not your aptitude, that will determine your altitude.

—Zig Ziglar

The Magic

ACRONYMS, FORMULAS, & IMPACTFUL STORIES

of Leadership

A Tribute to the Amazing Dr. Rob Gilbert *& the Success Hotline*

EXTREME

"***Extreme" is Dr. Gilbert's one-word seminar*** on success. Out of all his 12,500 messages (as of April 2025), this is his one word: **EXTREME.** Whatever it is that you want to do in life, be extreme about it. Throughout the next eight chapters of this book, you will read dozens of tips and strategies about being successful in your life. This is Dr. Gilbert's one word. He says it will be on his tombstone. The most important word: Extreme.

So, as we start this journey together of *The Magic Acronyms, Formulas, and Impactful Stories*, in dedicating the book to Dr. Rob, I ask you: What are you extreme about? What do you *want* to be extreme about?

Dr. Gilbert does this exercise in his freshman seminar class each year. He gives students an index card. He asks them to write down everything that they really want in life—that they *really* want. It can be anything: money, fame, travel, careers, etc.

After giving them some time to complete the assignment, he then asks, "Now, what is it you ***really, really*** want?" He asks them to circle those items and think about it/them. Then he shares one of his famous quotes from his wrestling coach at the University of Massachusetts that hung on the wall in the wrestling room. It read: "If you *really* want to be a champion, then the work is no problem." Doc has shared this quote many times over the years on the Hotline, and he focuses on the word *really*. If you *really* want something, you have to be *extreme* about it, and that is what many parts of this book are about: deciding on the person you want to be and then becoming that person. Be *extreme* about it! FOCUS on it: **f**ollow **o**nly **o**ne **c**ourse **u**ntil **s**uccessful (Chapter 5), and, as Nike and Dr. Gilbert say, Just do it!

Doc offers these strategies to get started:

1. Find out who you want to be/what you want. You can complete the exercise above.
2. Find out who the person is that you want to be or who has what you want to have.
3. Find out their strategies, habits, and techniques.
4. Start. Like I wrote in the previous paragraph: Just do it!

I recommend doing this card activity as you read the book. As you read the different excerpts, stories, and strategies in the book, go back to the card. Do your goals change? Do the things you want change?

Do this activity again at the end of the book, and then follow the strategies listed above. *Success leaves clues*—another Dr. Gilbert gem (Chapter 3), and the people are out there to help you. There is also this thing called YouTube. I heard that it can be helpful in learning how to do things and figuring things out. Go for it! The Success Hotline community will be here to support you on your journey. Good luck, and I hope you enjoy the book and the tribute to Dr. Gilbert for all he has done for so many.

FROM THE SUCCESS HOTLINE ARCHIVES . . .

Dr. Rob: If you think that it's going to be difficult
to be extreme, imagine how difficult
it will be to compete against
a person who is extreme
if you're not!

For example . . .

Passion Persuades

Many years ago, a rich gem collector came to Harry Winston's jewelry store in New York City. A salesman spent more than an hour trying to sell him a million-dollar diamond. No sale.

The collector was walking out the door when Mr. Winston stopped him. "Sir, can I have a moment with you?" Mr. Winston asked.

The two men went to Mr. Winston's office with the gem. After just 15 minutes, the collector decided to buy it. After paying for it, he asked Mr. Winston if the original salesman was any good. "He's the most knowledgeable person in the industry," bragged the owner.

"Then why couldn't he close the sale like you?" asked the collector.

Mr. Winston thought for a moment and said, "There's one big difference between the two of us: He *knows* diamonds, but I *love* diamonds!"

That type of passion is *extreme.*

– Do more than expected. –

■ ■ ■

HUNGRY

You've got to be hungry. Dr. Gilbert has shown this famous motivational video by Les Brown many times in his classes and seminars. You can find the video easily on YouTube by searching "Les Brown: You've got to be hungry."

It really sums up many of Doc's messages and points about *making it happen* in your life. I won't give the whole speech, so that you can enjoy watching the video. Les tells the story about wanting to become a DJ—a disc jockey, playing music on the radio. He goes through all the *no's* he receives on the journey, until he finally receives a *yes* in a funny and memorable way. I love this line from the video: *"It is better to be prepared for an opportunity and not have one than to have an opportunity and not be prepared."*

When you can focus on that one thing that you *really* want, as Doc has said many, many times on the Hotline, *you know what you want*. This simplifies things and allows you to go after it. You are less likely to be pulled away by distractions or other pursuits. Instead, pursue that goal, that position, that job, that speaking gig, etc., that you've always wanted.

Les exemplifies this point and more in this amazing video. I highly recommend that you spend five minutes watching it. He is passionate and enthusiastic, and a great storyteller—three important ingredients to Doc Gilbert's many recipes for success. *You've got to be hungry!* What is that ____ that you really want? Go get it!

FROM THE SUCCESS HOTLINE ARCHIVES . . .

"Wanting something is not enough. You must hunger for it. Your motivation must be absolutely compelling in order to overcome the obstacles that will invariably come your way."

—Les Brown, motivational speaker

– You are sitting on a gold mine.
When are you going to start digging? –

■ ■ ■

PRIDE

We all want to be proud of the work we are doing and have pride in our organizations, schools, and in other settings. There is satisfaction and fulfillment in knowing you have helped cultivate that pride within your teams. Can we define it? Can we put an acronym to it? Of course. Isn't that the name of this book? I'm not sure if it was Dr. Gilbert, Hall of Fame High School Basketball Coach Bobby Hurley, or another leader who created it. **PRIDE** is an acronym that stands for *positive mental attitude, repetition, imitation, determination, and enthusiasm.*

Positive mental attitude: Nothing bad can come from being positive. There is so much negativity out there. Why not try to find the positive? Think of the simple three-letter word "Yet" (in this book). *I can do it* or I can't do it **yet**. What a huge difference—and a positive one! What about the word "How"? During the pandemic of the 2020s, I was a high school principal in the great small city of Port Jervis, New York. There were many, many things we had to cancel, postpone, and change during that time. People were exhausted. People were very negative. We started to use the word *how* in our brainstorming. Not that we *couldn't* do something, but how *could* we do it with the Covid restrictions?

A dance was one good example from that tough time of the pandemic. *Can't have a dance,* we were told. We changed our mindset to *How* ***can*** *we have a dance?* We did it outside. We did it with circle pods. We did it by having a positive mental attitude.

Repetition and imitation: Keep doing something over and over until you get there. Look to see who **is** doing it right. See what they are doing, how they are doing it, and then *you* go do it. Sounds simple. Dr. Gilbert has said many times, "Success leaves clues." Who are those people, companies, or programs—that are doing the thing you want? Look for them, and just start doing what they're doing!

In *Outliers,* the great Malcolm Gladwell shared the story of how The Beatles got started in the '60s. They moved to Germany in 1960 and signed on to play at a 24-hour Rock club for 8-hour shifts. Playing music for 8 hours! They did this for four years, honing their skills, and certainly repeating their craft over and over—they *really* exemplified the 10,000 rule and concept of repetition.

Determination: Dr. Gilbert said over and over: If you *really* want something, then the work is no problem. Many concepts in this book come down to determination, will, and *really.* If you are determined to keep going, then you will. Doc shared the story of the man whose daughter needed a kidney transplant. Without one, she was given six to eight months to live. The father was a perfect match, yet he was overweight. He needed to lose more than one hundred pounds to be eligible to donate a kidney. That is a tough goal to reach in six months or so.

Determination: the father was determined to lose the weight and did so in three months; he donated the kidney to his daughter, saving her life. If you *really* want something, then the work is no problem. If you are determined, then nothing can stop you.

Lastly, enthusiasm. The great American author Ralph Waldo Emerson famously wrote, "Nothing great was accomplished without enthusiasm." It is free, doesn't require training, and creates joy. I feel enthusiasm is so important on our journey that I made it part of my logo and my journey of inspiring others.

Of all the ingredients of success contained within this book, enthusiasm is one of the most important. Make sure you include it in your recipe.

FROM THE SUCCESS HOTLINE ARCHIVES . . .

Success Hotline Message #10,120

Dr. Rob: The people you're working with, the people you're teaching, the people you're coaching, the people you're leading—*do they believe that you believe*? That's where greatness and magic happen—when they believe that you believe. Because if they believe that you believe, then they might start believing it, too! For example, if you're an English teacher and you believe that Shakespeare was the greatest writer ever to walk the Earth, then your students might start believing it, too. Many times, they won't believe it until they believe that you believe it.

Believing is not something that can be *taught*—it must be *caught*!

This might also be called "enthusiasm." Look at the last four letters of that word: IASM. That's an acronym that stands for I AM SOLD MYSELF. In other words, "I totally believe that I believe." That's where greatness begins. If sales is "believing something and convincing others," it all begins with selling yourself, buying yourself, and believing that you believe.

▪ ▪ ▪

~Nothing can stop the person with the right mental attitude from achieving their goal. Nothing on earth can help a person with the wrong mental attitude.~

~Thomas Jefferson, 3rd President of the United States~

ACT AS IF

by Mark Glicini, Ph.D.

Mark is a standout professional lacrosse player, a Certified Fitness Trainer, Nutritionist, and Mental Performance Coach. He is a graduate of Yale University and a New Jersey native. He is a loyal, longtime caller of the Success Hotline. Mark is an incredible speaker, motivator, and person looking to make a positive impact on the world. He is a leading authority and author in the field of Applied Sport Psychology. You can learn more about Mark here: https://www.markglicini.com/

▪

Sometimes, we smile because we're happy, and, sometimes, we are happy because we smile. Through our body language, behavior, and actions, we take control of our own internal mental state, which allows us to thrive under pressure.

Young athletes want more confidence, and professional athletes want greater consistency. As a mental-performance coach, I encourage both confidence and consistency to practice the disciplines that strengthen those intangibles. Both confidence and consistency come from repetitions. The question is: What kind of repetitions?

Due to inexperience, a young athlete must embody the physical training of a certain craft. He or she has only a fraction of the necessary hours invested into a sport. Mastery requires muscle memory, and it starts with the physical, kinesthetic feel of going through the physiological motions with appropriate intensity. Physical training, after thousands of hours, leads to self-perceived data that overcomes doubt.

Once the physical discipline is instilled, emotional fitness and mental training become paramount. How do athletes speak to themselves? What does an athlete focus on? Who do they choose to surround themselves with? Overwhelming feelings and lack of focus have the power to interfere with physical performance. The difference maker between good and great athletes: cultivating habits that put an athlete's inner world in a state of ease and peace.

What fires together, in the brain, wires together. We become what we do most of the time. Excellence is a byproduct of healthy actions stacked on top of one another for years. Mastery manifests after many, many, many hours of training. Peak performers start with pretending, progress through failing, and achieve by acting. *Acting as if* they can. *Acting as if* they will. *Acting as if* they deserve it.

Into action: When you feel small, act big. A bigger presence leads to a greater capacity to perform, especially under pressure.

Commit to healthy actions, and you will be amazed at the outcomes that follow.

Next time you enter your arena of performance, act bigger than you feel. Next time you find yourself wondering how someone else accomplished something truly remarkable, remind yourself that it's the result of years of training, and get back to the work. When you hear that voice in your head that says, "You can't; you're not good enough," TAKE ACTION and *act as if.*

FROM THE SUCCESS HOTLINE ARCHIVES . . .

The World's Most Confident Fourth-Grader

Dr. Rob: Once there was a young girl who thought she could do anything, and when she couldn't, she acted as if she could!

No one else thought that she was the smartest fourth-grader. And no one else ever said that she was the most musical, the most athletic, or the most artistic.

But this little girl was the world's most *confident* fourth-grader, because she thought that she could do absolutely anything.

One day, the art teacher came into class and said, "Today you can paint or draw anything you want."

The world's most confident fourth-grader shot her hand up into the air and asked, "Can I draw a picture of God?"

Through her smile, the teacher said, "Nobody's quite sure what God looks like."

With all the confidence in the world, the little girl said, "Oh, they will when I'm done!"

The world's most confident fourth-grader's message to you:

~Act as if it were impossible to fail.~

■ ■ ■

C > F = R

by Jove Stickel

Jove Stickel has served as an educator in Missouri for nearly 30 years. He started as a social-studies teacher, coaching wrestling, track, and football; now, he serves as a middle school principal. He had always taken care of others and was focused on leading those around him but struggled to lead himself. In 2020, he decided it was time to make a change and start leading not just others but also himself. He went from weighing in at more than 600 pounds to losing 332 pounds and becoming the regional principal of the year.

▪

There are moments in life that are so impactful, so defining that you are transformed forever. That is exactly how I felt the first time I heard Dr. Gilbert say, "When your commitment is greater than your feelings, you get results (C > F = R)." This formula is the core belief that would change my thinking in a way I could've never imagined. I started listening to the Success Hotline in the spring of 2021, and, by late summer, my mindset had been shifted by the formulas, acronyms, and stories Dr. Gilbert shared every day. In just two years, I went from being a 600-pound bariatric patient to a middle school principal of the year who is on a 1000+ day running streak. In this excerpt, I share how Dr. Gilbert's message became my superpower in overcoming my mental roadblocks.

When your commitment is greater than your feelings, you get results. I adopted this as my life's mantra. This tiny formula—*C > F = R*—is so ingrained in my everyday life that it's on a sticker on the back window of my truck. It's my tagline in my morning messages. It's the focus of my podcast, and it's forever tattooed on my right wrist. This formula is life! Everything in life—and I mean *everything*—can come back to C > F = R.

There is no limit to what I can achieve if I apply this formula with fidelity in all that I do. For years, I was told that, if you want success, there is no magic bullet; it is about hard work. I can say today with absolute certainty that many people work hard every day but never achieve the success they want because they *aren't committed to an extreme level.* To truly be committed, you must be extreme. Your commitment must not be denied or derailed by shiny objects, bells, whistles, or feelings. When you are truly committed, the odds don't matter because, eventually, you will achieve success. When you live a committed life, you are steadfast in the routines and procedures you develop to get the results you desire.

When you're committed, you must be willing to sacrifice comfort in the short term for what you want in the future. You must be willing to stay home when your friends want to stay out late and party, because you have an early-morning run that you won't miss. Your present feelings are not as important as your commitment and the results you wish to attain. One of the ways I explain this comes from the world of sports. How many times have you heard a coach or a parent in a close game say, "You gotta *want* it." The truth is that *everybody* wants it, but how committed have you been to getting it? The person who is willing to put their feelings aside will win more often than not. That person is the person who works out *even when they don't feel like it.* Those people will do more than is expected of them because they know it is good for them. Those people will eat the right foods, even though they *want* to scarf down an entire bag of chips.

C > F = R is one of the most basic philosophies to follow in the world. It isn't magic; it isn't complicated; it is, however, determination, discipline, hard work, sacrifice, and courage rolled into one life-changing phrase. C > F = R has become the core value around which my world revolves. It applies to my running, my career, my relationships with others, my financial stability, and my nutrition. There is no end to what C > F = R can be applied to.

CALL TO ACTION

I want you to take a minute and think of anything you have ever worked for in your life—things you have achieved *and* things that you have fallen short of attaining. Now ask yourself: Could I have achieved those things—and more—if my commitment had been greater than my feelings? Think about how your feelings derailed your attempt at success. Starting right now, not tomorrow or next week, I challenge you to pick out a goal—big or small—and I want you to become extremely and totally committed to getting results.

FROM THE SUCCESS HOTLINE ARCHIVES . . .

"A commitment is doing what you said you would do long after the feeling you had when you said it has passed."

"A pro is the person who has all the hassles, obstacles, disappointments, and frustrations that others have, yet continues to persist, does the job, and makes it look easy!"

~David Cooper, sales trainer extraordinaire

DWYSYWD

Do What You Say You Will Do.

AC-CC-PH

I'd like to thank JD Collins for sharing this concept. JD is the former National Coordinator of the NCAA Men's Basketball Officials. For non-basketball fans, he is the gentleman that selected the officials for the March Madness basketball tournament. I had a chance to interview JD on my leadership podcast, entitled #ELB: **E**ducation **L**eadership and **B**eyond Podcast.

You can view that interview here: https://bit.ly/ELBpodcastJD Collins

He was also generous enough to write an excerpt in one of my previous books, *Tales from the Hardwood.* When I asked *him* to describe the job of an official in today's world, he answered with this: *absorb chaos, create calm, and provide hope.* What an incredible answer!!!

Whether you are an educator or whatever the field you're in, many times in our lives, it feels like that—we absorb chaos, create calm, and provide hope. Certainly, as a parent of teenagers, that is part of our role. I loved his answer so much that it became the last chapter in *Tales from the Hardwood* and a mainstay in my leadership presentations. Sometimes we tell ourselves, *This isn't what I signed up for. Why am I doing this?* When there's a food fight in the cafeteria and I'm cleaning up the meatballs off the wall, I would ask myself, *Why am I doing this?* The answer is ***because that's my job description: absorb chaos, create calm, and provide hope.***

There have been countless stories and moments in my life, as a school leader, parent, or men's college basketball official where I was presented with a situation that caused me to reflect back to this mindset of absorbing chaos, creating calm, and providing hope. Obviously, *whatever* field you were in during the time of the Covid pandemic, this was certainly the case. When you think back to this job description, it reminds you, "Yes, this is all part of the job." Keep doing it, my friends. We need you. We need you at your best, and this mindset helps you get through the hard times. AC-CC-PH: ***absorb chaos, create calm, and provide hope.***

FROM THE SUCCESS HOTLINE ARCHIVES . . .

HOPE = **H**ave **O**nly **P**ositive **E**xpectations
HOPE = **H**old **O**n! **P**ossibilities **E**xist
HOPE = **H**elp **O**ther **P**eople **E**xcel
HOPE = **H**old **O**n! **P**ain **E**nds

■ ■ ■

~Winners are not passionate because they are successful. They are successful because they are passionate.~

GET YOUR PHD

S*o, have you watched* the video *You Gotta Be Hungry,* by Les Brown, yet? What are you waiting for? This book and Dr. Gilbert's message are all about taking action. If you want to do it right now with your phone, you can scan the QR code here to view *You Gotta Be Hungry* by Les Brown:

Are you ready for a breakthrough on your journey? *Get your PH.D.* Are you looking to make the next step? *Get your PH.D.* You want to complete that project you've been working on, that doctorate degree? Maybe you should get your PH.D. instead:

POSITIVE, HUNGRY, AND DETERMINED

When you live these three traits, you can't lose. Trying to reach that goal? Bring your PH.D. Get turned down for that promotion? Bring your PH.D. Be **p**ositive, **h**ungry, and **d**etermined. I love how Les tells the story and yells enthusiastically, "You gotta be **HUNGRY!**" It leaves no doubt about how to show up and be ready for that opportunity, and if you stay P-H-D, when the opportunity comes, you will be ready! Stay *hungry,* friends!

FROM THE SUCCESS HOTLINE ARCHIVES . . .

Dr. Rob: Many people believe that it takes *intelligence* to earn a Ph.D.

Absolutely false.

More important than intelligence is diligence.

In the world of academia, diligence beats intelligence every single time!

Absolutely! Positively!! Guaranteed!!!

~Things work out best for those who make the best of the way things work out.~

▪ ▪ ▪

CHAPTER 2

MINDSET

If you fail—or if you're not the best—it's all been wasted. The growth mindset allows people to value what they're doing, regardless of the outcome.

~CAROL DWECK

The Magic
ACRONYMS, FORMULAS, & IMPACTFUL STORIES
of Leadership

A Tribute to the Amazing Dr. Rob Gilbert
& the Success Hotline

INTO IT

T*his is a Dr. Gilbert favorite.* Many, many times on the Hotline, at seminars, and at conferences, he has posed this all-important question, "Are you in it, or ***into it***?" Whatever it is in your life—your school, your job, your team—are you just *in it* or ***into*** it? There is a big difference.

Into means enthusiasm, excitement, and "I want to be here and do an amazing job at this thing at this very moment." The great Ralph Waldo Emerson said that *nothing great was ever accomplished without enthusiasm.* The great Dr. Gilbert says, *"Be **into** it"* if you want to be great at something.

On the Hotline, he talks about the classes he teaches often—both when his students are super excited about class *and* when they are less than enthused.

He shared this story on the Hotline: He told the class that he was having a guest in class who was a talent scout for Broadway shows. They were looking for someone to play the role of an enthused student in a college classroom—raising their hand, making eye contact with the professor, engaging with classmates, taking notes, etc. If they were selected by the agent, they would land a job on Broadway acting in the musical, making thousands of dollars per month, and living the life of a Broadway star. Could they—would they—do it? *Sure* they would, if this were indeed true. Yet, they know it is ***not*** true, so they don't *act* that way.

What Dr. Gilbert has tried to convey while teaching and running the Hotline for 30+ years is that *you become the way you act.* When you act enthused, *you become enthusiastic.* When you act ***into*** it, you *become engaged, focused, and actually* ***into*** what you are a part of.

I am very proud to hang a sign in my school district that reads: "Don't just be in school—be ***into*** school." When we make ourselves be ***into*** something, we become just that.

So, what is it for you? Your partner, spouse, family, job, book writing, running marathons? What is it? Take five minutes now, and write down on a piece of paper or notes on your phone: What is it you are ***into*** or want to be ***into***, and how are you ***into*** it? Then, make a second list—what more could you be doing, or stop doing, or do differently to be ***more into*** whatever it is you want to do. It works; trust me.

Here are three things that take absolutely zero talent or training that can help you be more ***into*** whatever it is you want. You can do them with ease. You just have to make them a priority and focus on doing them.

1. *Wear the gear of your team, organization, or family.* As I write this, I am in my 22nd year at Port Jervis Schools. I love it there—the people, the community, and the work. I am now at the point where I could wear a different Port shirt for almost a year without repeating it. I have collared shirts, button-down shirts, t-shirts, sweatshirts, hoodies, sport coats, winter jackets, and hats. You name it, I have it with *Port* on it. I ***want*** to carry the banner for Port schools and be ***into*** it. Putting on the gear is like putting on my uniform—ready for the work, the school day. It is a badge of honor, a badge of Port Pride. It really sets in when I go somewhere else, and someone asks, "You work at Port?" *You're dang right I do, and I'm proud of it.* I am ***into*** it, and wearing the gear helps me do that. Zero talent—just focus and intention.

2. *Be early to meetings, events, and games.* When you are early, it shows you care, and when you're ***into*** things, you care about them. Also, early is magic time. It allows for a few things to happen naturally. First, it allows you to talk with others about

what you're there for. It gives you a few minutes to catch your breath and have some relaxed conversation. It gives you time to build relationships. When you are ***into*** it, you can share with others about your enthusiasm for that *person, etc.* you are into. You are prepared. You are ready.

Imagine in your head that you are at that great movie or show. What does that person look like/feel like when they are rushing in late to the event? They are flustered, frustrated, and not at their best. When you're early, you are prepared and set up to be ***into*** it. I know that things happen that throw you off schedule at times. I am talking about the norm, not the exception.

Here is an excerpt from a testimonial letter from my friend Darren Moran. Darren and I refereed many years together with the New York CBOA (College Basketball Officials Association), and he had me in to speak to his referee group, IAABO Board 52, in New York. I was thrilled to see that Darren noticed my intentionality in arriving early and the good things that come from being early:

This year, the executive committee decided to have Andrew as our keynote speaker, and he did not disappoint! Andrew arrived at the dinner an hour early to set up his laptop for the slideshow and to check the sound system. Andrew also took the time to chat with the members as they arrived. Andrew's presentation was passionate, informative, and inspirational.

Again, being early takes zero talent—only Focus and Intention.

3. *Serve others.* At the conclusion of this book, I write, "It's about others." Dr. Gilbert's whole message on the Hotline

is about helping others. He inspires, encourages, motivates, and makes others feel special, as the great Ed Agresta wrote in this book. When you are ***into*** it, you want to uplift others and make them feel good. You're feeling good, and you're ***into*** it, so you look to uplift and deposit into the lives of others. Your bucket is full, so you can fill the buckets of others.

There are three simple ways to do this: *1. Ask people about themselves.* And not just the classic greeting, "How you doin'?" where people don't even stick around to hear or care about the answer, especially in the Northeast. Be specific. How is your Mom? How did that meeting go for you? Update me on your kids—they're amazing like you. Ask about them, and be specific.

4. *Offer a compliment.* Don't be fake and make something up; find something positive to say. Many people comment on people's clothes or appearance. I challenge you to go deeper. Find something good and positive about that person. When you consistently look for the good in others, you can find it. This also helps you be ***into*** being positive, searching for the good in others. Additionally, it helps you look past the not-so-great things about people. This enthuses *you* as well as the receiver of your comments.

When I was in high school and college, I worked as a summer basketball camp counselor. I loved it. This experience made me want to become a teacher. On each Thursday of camp (camp ended on Friday), I'd have to write 13 report cards for my campers—and find something positive to say. Even if the kid didn't make a shot all week and couldn't dribble, I'd dig deep and ***find something positive*** to say: "You were a great teammate this week." "You have an awesome attitude." "I loved your hustle on and off the court!" When you look hard enough for the positive, you will find it.

Finally, 3. *Ask the question, "How can I help?"* I remember cleaning in the kitchen one day, feeling good that I was helping my wife out with the household chores. I could sense she was getting frustrated with me. I thought, *How could that be? I'm helping her.*

After giving her a little space, I returned and asked, "Did I do something wrong? Was I bothering you in some way?" Her answer changed our marriage for the better in a great way. She answered, "Andrew, I know you were trying to be helpful, and you meant well, but please, just ask the question: How can I help you?" When you ask this question, you can really find out what that person needs and maybe what they *don't* need. "How can I help you?" It's simple and direct, and it takes no talent. Make sure you listen for the answer!

OK—the next piece of homework is to watch the 2009 movie *Julie & Julia.* This is the true story of Julie Powell, the self-made chef and author. She decided to cook one of the famous chef Julia Child's recipes every day for a whole year and then blog about it. She was neither a chef nor a writer, but she ***got into*** both.

So, what comes first—the chicken or the egg? The passion or the success? How many times in our lives have we said, "I'll do that when I_______," and you could add a number of different endings to that sentence. She got really good at both by doing them each day. She got ***into*** it.

Her story is similar to Dr. Gilbert's. He just started to leave these messages, not knowing where it was going to go. He was just committed and ***into*** it. And here we are. Maybe one day, Doc's story will land on the big screen like *Julie & Julia* did. Who knows? For now, we've got the *Magic Acronyms, Formulas, and Stories of Leadership* in honor of the truly amazing Dr. Rob!

FROM THE SUCCESS HOTLINE ARCHIVES . . .

The Most Important Decision You'll Ever Make

Dr. Rob: What's the most important decision that you'll ever make?

Is it where you will go to school?
Is it what job you should take?
Is it whom you will marry?

All these decisions are important, maybe even life-changing, but none of these decisions is the #1 most important decision you'll ever make.

Did you ever realize that there's a ***big*** difference between just *going to school* and *being a student*?

Did you ever realize that there's a ***big*** difference between just *playing a sport* and *being an athlete*?

Did you ever realize that there's a ***big*** difference between just *singing a song* and *being a singer*?

What's the point?

The most important decision you'll ever make is:

Are you going to be

in it

or

into it?

Are you going to be ***in*** school or ***into*** school?
Are you going to be ***in*** your job or ***into*** your job?
Are you going to be ***in*** a relationship or ***into*** your relationship?

If you're "in school"—you're enrolled.
If you're "into school"—you're involved.

If you're "in a job"—you have a boss.
If you're "into your job"—you are a boss.

If you're "in a relationship"—you're headed for trouble.
If you're "into a relationship"—you're happy.

If you can *decide to be more* ***into it*** *right now*—you've taken your first step on your road to success.

Absolutely! Positively!! Guaranteed!!!

"***Into it***" athletes are winners, champions, and gold medalists.

The most "***into it***" performance I have ever seen in the Olympics was by two British ice dancers named Torvill and Dean. Check them out on YouTube.

~Luck is when preparation meets opportunity.~

▪ ▪ ▪

STSS

D*r. Gilbert often says* that successful people talk to themselves frequently. Sounds weird, right? As kids, we were told that people who talk to themselves are crazy. Well, here in the *Magic Acronyms, Formulas, and Impactful Stories of Leadership* book, that is not the case. We *are* going to define it, though—with an acronym, of course: STSS. It has two meanings, one positive and one negative. As always, let's start with the positive. Being positive should always be put first and should always be at the forefront of our minds and decision-making.

STSS: **S**tart **T**elling **S**uccessful **S**tories. The stories we tell ourselves are the ones that we will do and live. I love movies with great positive stories. I love amazing true-inspiration stories that uplift and motivate us. We say to ourselves, "Wow, that is incredible!" *Rudy* and *The Miracle on Ice* are two stories that jumped out at me and were made into movies—both wonderful, heartfelt stories of overcoming adversity and doing what others said was impossible. If you haven't seen them, OMG, you must! They are fantastic. I love them because they make me want to do (what *others* might think—***not me***!) the impossible. They make me tell myself a successful story. They deliver it right to us on the big screen. We don't have to research them or go hunting for them. They are right there, at the movies! It's so easy to find success stories.

Here's another story that I hope makes it to the big screen one day. It is the real-life story of my friend Paul Babcock, a faithful

Success Hotline caller who wrote the book *The Team*. You don't have to be a baseball fan to fall in love with this book and Paul's story. It is an all-American, hard-working story of triumph and victory through failure and struggle. I'll anxiously await a movie with a storyline similar to the movie *Rudy*.

Paul shares anecdotes and stories of growing up with a large family on a farm in Illinois. He was the youngest child, constantly getting dumped on to do this and that. Being the youngest myself, I can relate. Paul went on to play baseball for the College of St. Francis (now the University of St. Francis) in the NAIA (National Association of Intercollegiate Athletics—the NCAA before the NCAA existed) in Illinois.

After his sophomore year, the coaches told Paul he would never play again and thanked him for his dedication. They basically offered him an invitation to leave the team. Paul said he understood but still wanted to be part of the team and asked where he could be an impact player, perhaps as a pinch runner, etc. Paul was in great shape, very fast, and dedicated to helping the team improve.

Most people, when told they have zero chance to play again, would take their ball and glove and go home. They flat-out told him he wouldn't play again. Paul remained positive. He continued to give his all and had a good attitude. He STSS'd!—started telling success stories. His story was that he would remain positive and ***remain on the team*** despite being told he would not play again.

During his junior year, what they told him was true. He didn't play, but he continued with his positive attitude. He still showed up at practice and gave it his all. He continued STSS.

However, during his senior year, things changed. A couple of players had transferred. Paul's continued dedication to showing up and working hard earned him an opportunity to play in the outfield, and he became a starter.

The team went on to make it to the College World Series, and Paul became a full-time player and contributor. Below and on the QR code is a clip of Paul making a diving catch in the World Series game that helped Saint Francis win the championship.

View here: https://bit.ly/ELBlogBabcockcatch

It's unbelievable. Going from a kid who was being told he was not going to play to making a World Series game-saving catch with immense effort on this play is just incredible. Kudos to Paul for SSTS on his journey! Paul's book *The Team* is both in print and on Audible, with himself as the narrator.

~HOPE: **H**old **O**n! **P**ossibilities **E**xist~

FROM THE SUCCESS HOTLINE ARCHIVES . . .

Dr. Rob: One of the questions on my Sport Psychology final exam is, "What is the #1 most powerful story in the world?" The answer may surprise you! The #1 most powerful story in the world is the story you keep telling yourself over and over again. Since we become what we think about most of the time, we also become the stories we tell ourselves over and over again. Once you STSS (**S**tart **T**elling **S**uccessful **S**tories), your life is going to dramatically improve! Absolutely! Positively!! Guaranteed!!!

~If you want to be a champion tomorrow,
start acting like one today!
~Dr. Rob Gilbert

▪ ▪ ▪

ACT LIKE YOUR MOM IS WATCHING

When I officiated college basketball, I always loved it when my Mom watched the games. I liked it even more when she was in the stands at the event. I reffed better. I was more active and wanted to do a better job, knowing that my Mom was watching. Here are some pictures of Mom at some of the games.

Years later, I reflected on the phenomenon I experienced when my Mom watched the games. Why did I feel the need to ref better, run harder, and perform better overall? Why was this?

It was easy. *I wanted to make my Mom proud.* I wanted her to feel, in her heart and mind, that, *Wow! That is my boy out there.* I wanted her to be proud of me.

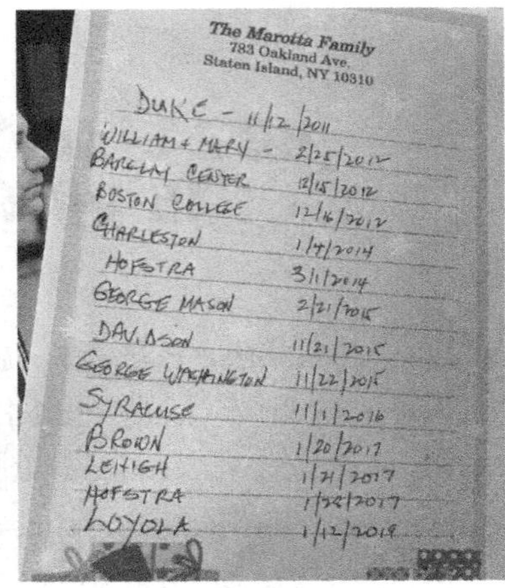

So why tell this story in the magic-acronym book? Why? I challenge you to ***act as if your Mom is watching.*** Act like Mom is watching you at work, at school, when you are at your best, and when you are at your worst. I was better knowing my Mom was watching. I share this story often when I speak publicly. I can see it tug at people's hearts and minds as they reflect on their relationships with their Moms. Try it—your Mom will be/would be proud.

I wanted to make my parents proud of me, and the work I was doing was always important to me. Even as a youngster, whether it was doing my paper route or completing an odd job at my neighbor's home, I knew, at some point, someone would comment to my parents on the job I was doing—and I wanted it to be a good comment. I wanted my parents to be proud of me.

Now, as a professional, this feeling is still true, and my Mom was actually watching me perform, so I wanted to do a good job even more. When you're working, *act as if* your Mom (or Dad) is watching you, and you'll do a better job!

FROM THE SUCCESS HOTLINE ARCHIVES . . .

Dr. Rob: Want to solve one of the great mysteries in all of sports? Here it is: How come, when a college football game is being broadcast on TV, and the camera is on the players on the bench, the players ***always*** say, "Hi, Mom!" I have ***never*** heard a "Hi, Dad!" Not once, not ever. Can you solve this mystery?

~You are what you think about most of the time.~

■ ■ ■

DON'T QUIT—CAN'T FAIL

D*on't quit—can't fail*. Don't quit—can't fail. Don't quit—can't fail. Say it over and over and over. Don't quit—can't fail. Don't quit—can't fail. Don't quit—can't fail. Whatever it is in your life—weight, goals, travel, speaking, leading, sports—this mantra is so true. Tell yourself, and it will be. There are so many examples of this in my life. Literally, over and over, if you just keep showing up, good things will happen.

Here are two examples that jump out at me: writing and podcasting. Both of these have become passions of mine. I had zero training when I started both. I just started. I started writing and podcasting. It was weird and uncomfortable. I felt a little unsure, yet I just went with my gut and kept doing them. When I was busy, I did a podcast. When I was tired, I wrote. When I didn't feel like doing either, I made time to do them and work at them. When I hit 300 podcasts, 300 blogs, and now my seventh book, I looked back and said, "Wow . . . how did *that* happen?" Now I know how it happened: *not quitting and just keeping at it.*

There are no secrets here. Just don't quit—can't fail. Don't quit—can't fail. Don't quit—can't fail. Don't quit—can't fail. What is it in your life that you want to succeed in? Write it down. Make it highly visible, and *don't quit*. Keep at it. Keep rolling through the ups and downs.

Be mindful on your journey of not quitting. This mindset, this action-based affirmation, *doesn't say:* "Don't change, don't adapt, and don't try new ways or new methods." Just keep trying, keep showing up, and keep working at it. Tweak, change, make progress, and *don't quit—can't fail.* Don't quit—can't fail. Don't quit—can't fail. I *love* this. Thanks, Doc!

FROM THE SUCCESS HOTLINE ARCHIVES . . .

WHO IS THIS???

Age 22:
Failed in business.
Age 23:
Lost in run for legislature.
Age 24:
Failed in business again.
Age 25:
Elected to legislature.
Age 26:
His sweetheart died.
Age 27:
Had a mental breakdown.
Age 29:
Defeated for Speaker.
Age 31:
Defeated for Elector.
Age 34:
Defeated for Congress.
Age 37:
Elected to Congress.

Age 39:
Defeated for Congress.
Age 46:
Defeated for Senate.
Age 47:
Defeated for Vice President.
Age 49:
Defeated for Senate.
Age 51:
Elected President.
Who was he???
Abraham Lincoln.
Setbacks are setups
for comebacks.
Setbacks were setups
for comebacks
for Abraham Lincoln.
Setbacks
will be setups
for comebacks for you, too!
You will fail.
When you bounce back
from your failures—
you'll succeed.
Abe did!

~Good, better, best. Never, ever rest, until your good gets better, and your better gets best.~

■ ■ ■

LOSE

I *was blessed growing up* to be pretty good at sports and pretty good at school. When I fell short in areas, I just worked harder to get to where I needed to be. It wasn't something I thought about much, and I just thought it was the way the world worked. I really wanted to get better at it, and if I wasn't passionate about it or just really not very good at it, I did something else and didn't put much thought to it.

I began to learn more about the concept of confidence and self-esteem. Dr. Gilbert has talked about this a lot over the years. As I advanced in my journey of leadership as a school administrator and as a college basketball official, things became more competitive. There were interviews, different games, and situations for which *many* people competed to be selected. This is when I started to *talk to myself* to work on my confidence, like building muscle in the weight room. I began to focus and prepare deeper and more thoroughly for these events, tryouts, and presentations.

I began to speak to myself to tell myself that I was good enough for these positions, as well as to visualize that I could do it. This process helped me with my confidence and self-esteem. The longer I'm around, the more I learn that this trait of strengthening your self-esteem and confidence is not that common. I see many people doubt themselves too much, and a lack of self-esteem creeps in. Their whispers and doubts dominate their confidence. That's the definition of lack of self-esteem. When you have LOSE, you continue to cycle downward. When you have a LOSE mentality, it can be hopeless in a lot of ways.

LOSE = **L**ack **O**f **S**elf-**E**steem

If you struggle with your self-esteem and confidence on your journey, start talking to yourself. There are many acronyms and things in here that can help with this. Try to change the LOSE mentality into confidence. **Tell yourself you can do it**: believe in yourself. Dress the part, look the part, and visualize yourself doing it.

Then you just have to face that fear, and do it. I use the example of doing pushups a lot. You look at fit people and say, "Wow, that's incredible. Look how lucky they are." You wish that you were more fit, but you have no idea how to do it. Start with one pushup. The next day, you'll have a second, and a third, and so on. In 30 days, you'll be able to do 30 pushups, and that is a long way from where you were.

Many people ask about writing books. Maybe they lack the self-esteem to do so. I had no idea how to write a book until Dr. Gilbert helped me believe that I could. He told me I should, and I just made a list of what I did as a principal. Once I had the list, I had the things I wanted to write about, and I literally just wrote about them.

Start writing a blog. Start out writing an article about a topic you are passionate about. These small victories help you move forward and help your self-esteem.

Add up the victories and they will begin to compound. A thin thread woven over and over becomes a thick, strong cord. Think about your confidence and self-esteem in this way, and they will grow–in the right direction. If you are losing or have LOSE, stop it right away, and start the things you want to grow in. I know it feels like it's easier said than done, but you can do it. I am challenging you—*just do it.* Act the way you want to become, and you will become the way you act.

~How to avoid criticism: Say nothing, do nothing, be nothing.~

■ ■ ■

I CAN DO THIS

2011 ***was my first year*** in the ACC (the Atlantic Coast Conference) as a men's college basketball official. I was thrilled for the opportunity and grateful to be working in such amazing venues and arenas. On November 12, 2011, I visited Duke University for the first time inside the historic Cameron Indoor Stadium. It happened to be the game in which Hall of Fame Coach Mike Krzyzewski (Coach K) was to tie the all-time record for wins by a Division I head college basketball coach. To say I was nervous would be an understatement. ESPN Primetime was broadcasting, there was a raucous crowd at Cameron Indoor, and I was just hoping to *survive*. We were about to step onto the floor to start the game, and my officiating partners handed me the ball to toss it up to start the game! *Really!* This kicked my anxiety up to the next level. I couldn't say "No," so I grabbed the ball and ran out on the court, trying to look confident but feeling totally nervous inside.

We were ready. It was time to toss the ball. Two giants were standing next to me at mid-court. Seven-foot monsters were ready to attack the game. I tossed the ball up as high as I could. My heart was blasting in my chest, slamming against my ribs, and my arms locked up—frozen like an old, rusty outdoor awning bracket in Maine in February!

I threw (I'm using that word loosely) the ball into the air, and it sailed sideways, like a failed rocket launch. I could hear the moans of the crowd, the grunting of the two jumpers (who expected the ball to shoot straight upward), and certainly the Hall of Fame Coach

K, yelling from the sideline. The whole place was like, "*What the _____?*" It was a disaster. I felt like a total failure in a very public moment—stinging, embarrassing, and paralyzing. Coach K was quoted after the game as saying, "It was the worst toss I've seen in my entire career!"

I survived the game, yet this terrible moment stuck with me. I couldn't shake it. In the next game, I shanked it *again*. This happened multiple times over the next couple of weeks. *I had to do something.*

I called Dr. Gilbert, looking for help. I shared what had happened and asked for advice on how I could work through it. He had the perfect solution. **I can do this. *I-Can-Do-This.*** Yes, his advice was that simple. I talked to myself by physically touching my fingers to my thumb. So, now, even though it was silently, I was talking to myself—*I can't toss the ball!*—as opposed to listening to myself—*I can't toss the ball. Try it. Let's do it together.*

Take your first finger or pointer finger, and touch it to your thumb and say, "I"; then touch your middle finger to your thumb and say, "can." Next, touch your ring finger to your thumb, and say, "do," and, lastly, touch your pinky to your thumb and say, "this." *I-can-do-this.* Dr. Gilbert taught me this short action affirmation after a tough setback in my life, *and it worked.* I was able to talk myself through it. The physical touching of my fingers to my thumb also helped. Over and over, I repeated this affirmation, telling myself I could do it—and guess what happened? *I did it.* I did it because I told myself I could—over and over and over.

I am very grateful to Dr. Gilbert for this amazing nugget—a great positive affirmation. I was able to talk myself through a tough situation with the perfect guidance from the great Dr. Rob.

FROM THE SUCCESS HOTLINE ARCHIVES . . .

Dr. Rob: "Repetition is the mother of learning." Repetition is also the mother of skill development. There are physical skills, and there are mental skills. If you want to get better at shooting a basketball—take a lot of shots. Repeat. Repeat. Repeat. If you want to have a better attitude and more confidence—do a lot of mental exercises. Repeat the ***I-Can-Do-This!*** exercise 250 times! Repeat! Repeat! Repeat! Will it work? Absolutely! Positively!! Guaranteed!!!

A journey of a thousand miles begins with one single step.

~Lao Tzu, Chinese Philosopher

■ ■ ■

BECAUSE OF THIS, SOMETHING GOOD WILL HAPPEN

Doc says this all the time on the hotline. This is one of those phrases we must tell ourselves when we talk to ourselves. Bad things happen all the time, and it is how we handle them that determines the outcome. It is our reaction (E + R = O, as explained in chapter 7) to these situations that will determine the outcome. *Because of this, something good will happen.* If we continue to remind ourselves of this mantra, this mindset, when things aren't going the way we want, it will help us continue to move forward. It is like searching for a reward, that lost item that is so valuable. It is no fun as you are looking until you find it. *Because of this, something good will happen.* A story:

The ACC: The Atlantic Coast Conference. I was a men's Division 1 college basketball official in the ACC for seven years and in various other Division 1 conferences over a span of twenty years. It was awesome. I loved it. I really enjoyed the ride and all the things that officiating brought to my life: focus, fitness, achievement, excellence, responsibility, and more.

The supervisor changed during my time in the ACC, and a new person took over. Soon after this change, I was released. I did not get a contract, and it was a tough blow for me. One of my first real rejections of 'not making it' in my life. I was quite down, but still trying to find the enjoyment in officiating.

This was right around the time when my first book came out, "*The Principal: Surviving & Thriving.*" The book was doing well, and I began to be asked if I presented leadership workshops and/or trainings. I hadn't yet, but I would answer, " Yes" without even having a presentation yet. That particular leadership group booked me, and off I went to create my first presentation.

The session was a hit, and they booked me again to speak later that same year. I began to do more presentations and less refereeing. I soon began to feel much greater satisfaction from giving inspiration and hope to others than blowing the whistle. The big-time basketball officiating was exhilarating, exciting, and challenging, yet helping others grow in their leadership was much more rewarding. *Who would have known?*

I eventually stepped away from officiating to dive into leadership speaking, presenting, coaching, and writing. ***Because of this, something good will happen***. At that time, I was saddened that I was let go from the ACC, frustrated with how it happened, and had a "woe is me" attitude. Yet this change happened simultaneously. One door closed, and the other opened right in front of me. Years later, I still shake my head at how it happened. I am passionate and dedicated to helping others on this leadership journey. If I had remained in the ACC, maybe this would have never happened. The mindset of "Because of this, something good will happen," carried me through this difficult time, opening doors to a whole new world for me of public speaking and writing—and here you are reading about it in this book!

FROM THE SUCCESS HOTLINE ARCHIVES . . .

Dr. Rob: Assignment—On YouTube, in this QR code, watch Garth Brooks singing "Unanswered Prayers."

~You drift toward the rocks. You sail toward success. If there is no wind, row!~

▪ ▪ ▪

CHAPTER 3

MOTIVATION

Don't wait to get motivated to do something.
Do something, and you'll get motivated.

The Magic
ACRONYMS, FORMULAS, & IMPACTFUL STORIES
of Leadership

A Tribute to the Amazing Dr. Rob Gilbert
& the Success Hotline

WHERE'S YOUR BOOK?

"*Where's your book?*" This is where it all started for me. After first meeting Dr. Gilbert and speaking in his class, he asked me, "*Where is your book?*" He told me he loved my presentation and that I needed to write a book. I told him there was *no way* and that I didn't know how. Then, he handed me ten books, and two of them were his. He told me *I could do it.* He enthusiastically urged me again, "You gotta write a book!" He shared that I didn't have to know *how*—just that I needed to write down the things I was doing as a principal, and that's the book.

Well, that's exactly what happened. I didn't text and drive, but I did talk-to-text on the way home from Montclair State University. In less than an hour, I had sixty points about being a principal recorded in the notes section of my phone. The next day at school, I had my notepad with me (one of the points in the book *The Principal*), and I wrote down forty more. In less than twenty-four hours of meeting Dr. Gilbert, I had 100 of the 125 learning points in my first book, *The Principal: Surviving & Thriving.* All because of Dr. Gilbert's urging, *motivating me to believe I could do it.*

Now, seven books later, I have fallen in love with writing and, more importantly, inspiring and motivating other people. Dr. Gilbert's direct and positive motivation of me transformed my life, literally. I went from being a Division I college basketball official to becoming a national speaker, all because he made me *believe I could be.* I continue to grow each and every day by calling the Success Hotline. It is challenging to describe the gratitude I feel toward Dr.

Rob and the amazing gift he has given me. *He changed my life* and helped me become my best self. I wake up daily wanting to inspire, to do more, be more, and continue to help others.

What is it for you? What is your book? And where is it? Get moving. Dr. Gilbert changed my life with his motivation, and I want this book to change yours!

FROM THE SUCCESS HOTLINE ARCHIVES . . .

Dr. Rob: Imagine a pie chart divided into three pieces: a 40% piece, another 40% piece, and a 20% piece. This is a pie chart about you! The first 40% piece is the things you know about yourself. The second 40% piece is the things you don't know about yourself. And the 20% piece are the things you don't know that you don't know about yourself. In this third piece, your gifts are right there, hiding in plain sight.

Sometimes it takes another person to introduce you to your greatest gifts!

~The purpose of life is to discover your gifts.
The meaning of life comes from giving your gifts away.~

~DR. DAVID VISCOTT, PSYCHIATRIST, AUTHOR, AND RADIO PERSONALITY~

■ ■ ■

GOYA

T*his excerpt is dedicated to* and inspired by the great Brian Cain. Brian is an amazing mental-performance coach and a #1 best-selling author who lives in Arizona. Brian shares the story of how Dr. Gilbert inspired him when he saw Gilbert speak at an athletic directors conference. Brian is a former high school athletic director from Vermont. After the session, Brian became inspired to be more and do more. Dr. Gilbert moved Brian in a way that changed his life. Dr. Gilbert pushed Brian to action and to GOYA: *Get Off Your Anatomy.*

Not only did Brian get off his anatomy and get moving to transform his life, but he also took it to the next level in many ways. Brian worked at it and stayed with it, and has become a leading expert in peak performance with college and professional athletes and major sports teams around the world. You can learn more about Brian here and also subscribe to his own version of the Success Hotline called "Mental Performance Daily" from the link below, or just do a quick Google search. Brian shares this every day, via iTunes, and it is awesome!

https://briancain.com/podcast-4

Dr. Gilbert has tremendously inspired me and so many others in a variety of ways. I see what Brian Cain has accomplished since meeting and spending time with Dr. Gilbert, and *Wow!* It makes me feel inspired and want to GOYA, too. Dr. Rob has become a mentor and friend to Brian, me, and many others. Brian really dove deep and has made a tremendous impact in the work he does inspiring athletes, teams, schools, and others. I highly recommend listening to his MPD Mental Performance Daily on iTunes each morning. I call the Success Hotline, listen to MPD, and then one last call, 'Talking with Terrie' (Chapter 8), daily. It is so great to hear and feel the impact not only from Dr. Gilbert every day, but also from two others who have gone on to make their own form of inspiration for others—of course, inspired by the great Dr. Rob Gilbert.

So, what is GOYA for you? What is that thing that makes you want to get off your anatomy and get started with? *Do it. Do it. Do it!* As we've shared throughout the book, get started. Need a boost to get moving? Call the Hotline or listen to a message from Brian Cain—*that* will *Get you Off Your Anatomy! You can follow him on Instagram here:* https://www.instagram.com/briancainpeak/?hl=en

FROM THE SUCCESS HOTLINE ARCHIVES . . .

Dr. Rob: The motivational speaker took out a $100 bill from his wallet, held it in the air, and said,
"Who wants this?"
Hands went up, and people yelled out,
"I do! I do!"
His next question was,
"Who *really* wants this?"
The hands went higher, and the yells got louder.
And then he waited . . .
until eventually someone jumped out of their chair,
ran up to the front of the room, and grabbed the bill

out of the speaker's hand.
What was the point?
The person who got
the money demonstrated
an important principle
of success: **GOYA**
The acronym **GOYA** = **G**et **O**ff **Y**our **A**natomy
Every person in that room
wanted the money.
But the money went
to the person who
got off their anatomy
and actually took action.
Everyone in that room could
have taken the money—but they didn't!
DOn't wa**IT**
GOYA

~Dominate the day.~
~Brian Cain

▪ ▪ ▪

SUCCESS LEAVES CLUES

by Randy Jackson

Randy Jackson is a former Texas high school head football coach who retired after a 33-year career. A three-time bestselling author—*Culture Defeats Strategy*, *Culture Defeats Strategy 2*, and his latest, *A Royal Season* (an Amazon international best-seller)—he is also a certified mental performance coach. Coach Jackson now develops mental performance and leadership curricula and consults full-time with athletic programs across the United States.

▪

S***uccess doesn't happen by chance.*** It's not about luck, nor is it an accident. Success leaves clues, and if you know where to look, you can fast-track your way to expertise by learning from those who have already figured out what works.

This idea was brilliantly illustrated by a former tennis teaching pro who became determined to become the world's leading authority on free-throw shooting in basketball. He was convinced that NBA free-throw shooting could be improved, and he knew he was the one to do it. However, like many readers of this book, he didn't know where to start, so he contacted Dr. Gilbert.

"Doc, I'm frustrated beyond belief every time I watch an NBA game, and the greatest athletes in the world barely make half of their foul shots. I want to be the guy who helps fix this."

Dr. Gilbert responded, "If you want to become the world's leading expert on free-throw shooting, you have two choices: spend

10,000 hours shooting them and working with all types of players, or call and interview those who already have done that."

This made sense to the tennis pro. "That's a terrific idea. I like that a lot."

Dr. Gilbert said, "Here's your first step: I have John Wooden's phone number. Call him and ask for his advice."

The tennis pro hesitated, doubting his ability to speak to such a legendary coach. "What? *Coach Wooden?* I can't do that," he said. "I'd be scared to death to speak with Coach Wooden. I'm sure he wouldn't speak to a nobody like me anyway."

Dr. Gilbert, ever persistent, encouraged him to overcome his fears and take action. Eventually, he made the call. To his surprise, Coach Wooden was gracious and offered priceless advice. He shared his knowledge and gave the tennis player phone numbers of other elite basketball coaches to reach out to.

The aspiring free-throw coach did just that. He called them all. He meticulously took notes, absorbed their expertise, and, over time, compiled all the lessons he had learned into a book on free-throw shooting. Then, his dream came true when he was hired to become the free-throw shooting coach for the Miami Heat!

The best part? Our tennis pro had never played a minute of basketball in his life! Success had left him a trail of clues, and he became an expert by following them.

This story illustrates a fundamental truth: ***Success leaves clues!***

Another example is Bill Belichick, arguably the greatest football coach ever. He claims to have the greatest football library in the world—a treasure trove of knowledge from past greats, and he's read them all. Phil Knight, the founder of Nike, holds his personal library in such high regard that he asks guests to remove their shoes before entering!

Warren Buffett is known for dedicating up to six hours a day to reading, constantly learning from the insights and experiences of others. This habit of absorbing vast amounts of information—from books, financial reports, and articles—has been a cornerstone of his success. By studying the strategies and wisdom of those who came before him, Buffett has refined his approach to investing and made informed, effective decisions. His commitment to learning from others is key to his legendary success.

There's no excuse for not becoming experts in our chosen fields. Whether your passion is basketball, baseball, investing, or any other domain, the resources are out there. The trail has already been blazed. Others have already done the work and want to share it with us!

If we GOYA, get off our anatomy (another Dr. Gilbert gem, from his tribute to Brian Cain), we can skip the 10,000 hours and go to the front of the line by learning from the greats who've toiled and already figured out what works and doesn't work.

If your passion is art, you don't need to spend decades learning the old-fashioned way. You can read books by the greatest artists who ever lived. You can watch tutorials from them on YouTube and emulate their techniques. You can grab a brush and paint "happy clouds" with Bob Ross right in your living room! The knowledge is available, and the shortcut to success is simple: learn from those who have done it before. The greats have left the clues, but it's up to you to take advantage of them.

Don't believe me? Still skeptical?

Then, here's your homework assignment: Become best friends with five elite individuals in your field. Let them be your mentors, helping you grow and become more. How do you do this? You research them. Years ago, I decided I wanted Pete Carroll, the current head coach of the Las Vegas Raiders, to mentor me. Though we'd never spoken, I read his books, took page after page of notes, and listened to every podcast and interview I could find. I essentially "stalked" Coach Carroll. His wisdom and insights have made me a better coach, even *without ever meeting him in person!*

One or two of your five mentors should be individuals you can speak with directly, people you can call, have lunch with, and ask questions. The other three can be experts you may never meet but whose knowledge is accessible through their work and public content.

We all have three choices:

1. *Stay where we are.*
2. *We can spend 10,000 hours trying to figure it out on our own.*
3. *Interview and learn from those who already have.*

Success leaves clues! I choose #3 every single time and highly recommend you do the same.

Dr. Gilbert, thank you for being one of my five mentors. You've made so many of us better by leaving mental-performance clues daily on the Success Hotline!

FROM THE SUCCESS HOTLINE ARCHIVES . . .

If you do what successful people have done, you'll get what successful people have gotten!

Dr. Rob: You can do anything anyone else can do, if you figure out how they did it—in other words, if you discover their strategies. As the great motivational speaker Tony Robbins has been saying for years, "Success leaves clues." If you study the lives of successful people, you will discover the "clues" or the strategies that made them so successful. This is not difficult! Most super-successful people in all fields have written books, and they tell you exactly what they did that led to their success. And YouTube is a virtual university of strategies. Whether you want to learn how to juggle or repair the bumper of your car, it's all on YouTube. Remember:

~If you do what successful people have done, you'll get what successful people have gotten!~

■ ■ ■

GOAL SETTING IN PLAYER AND TEAM DEVELOPMENT

by Maria Nolan

Maria Nolan just might be the greatest volleyball coach of all time! She was New Jersey's winningest high school volleyball coach, retired after 46 years with 1,101 wins, 116 losses, 30 State Championships, 10 Tournament of Champions, and 10 Gatorade Players of the Year.

She received numerous awards, including Disney's American Teacher Award, Frank McGuire Foundation, and the United Way, and was inducted into several Halls of Fame, including New Jersey State Interscholastic Athletic Association, New Jersey Scholastic Coaches Association, Hudson County, Secaucus High School, and Immaculate Heart Academy. Maria served the coaching community as a board member and past president of the National Federation of High Schools, the NFHS volleyball rules committee, along with many other committees for the NJSIAA.

▪

Little did I understand the importance and impact that meeting Dr. Rob Gilbert would have on my coaching career. It was in the 1980s that I first became acquainted with Dr. Gilbert and his approaches to success in sports. My first exposure was a two-day clinic he taught entitled "The Winner's Workshop." I followed this by taking a graduate-level course with him at Montclair State University. Dr. Gilbert presented many strategies that coaches could apply in pursuit of success. Throughout my career, I utilized several of his success strategies. The one that I believe had the greatest impact in my achieving success was goal-setting.

Through the years, reporters would ask, “How is it you produce winning teams year after year?” I learned that *confidence* was the most important factor.

While the answer was simple, it was something that had to be developed both within a player and within a team. Developing players’ confidence was a key element to our success, which was achieved through goal-setting. As each player gained confidence, our team became stronger and stronger. Often, I thought the outcome had been decided even before the match began. I knew if my players had enough confidence to beat the other team, they would.

Goal-setting became an integral part of my coaching planning. I would meet with a player every two weeks and ask, “What one thing do you want to improve upon?” Besides the player becoming aware of what needed to improve, it was also a “gentle” way of letting the player know her weakness. I would then suggest the one area I believed the player should improve. Usually, it was the same skill. I would be the deciding factor when we disagreed. After two weeks, if a player still needed improvement in that area, she would keep the same goal. In addition, this meeting was a good time to strengthen the player-coach bond by connecting with each other.

Early in my career, before taking Psychology of Sport, players would ask, “What do I need to improve?” After incorporating the principle of goal-setting, this question was rarely asked. Many times, coaches express frustration when players ask, “What do I need to improve?” since they give constant instruction and feedback during practices. Coaches would conclude there would be no need to ask. The importance of the instruction from a coach is often lost in the constant activity and distractions that occur during practices. However, in a goal-setting meeting, distractions are eliminated.

One of my favorite "confidence builders" was also learned in Dr. Gilbert's class.

A player was held accountable for getting better during every practice. At the end of practice, each player would say what she thought she'd improved on that day. If a player had trouble thinking of something, her teammates would be positive and help remind her of a great play, a breakthrough, or how she'd helped them. This was another way to build players' confidence. In addition, it was a terrific way for each player to realize how everyone was getting better, which, in turn, helped build team confidence. Perhaps an offshoot was the positive feedback they constantly gave each other. The players encouraged, cheered, and challenged each other not only during matches but also in practices. They wanted to stay on top and knew it meant each one of them had to keep improving.

I am forever grateful for the influence Rob had on my coaching career. He is responsible, too, for my many victories and championships.

FROM THE SUCCESS HOTLINE ARCHIVES . . .

Some Thoughts on Confidence

"Confidence is the most important single factor in this game, and no matter how great your natural talent, there is only one way to obtain it—work."

~Jack Nicklaus, superstar golfer

PREPARATION + CONFIDENCE = SUCCESS

~Paul Reddick, coach and entrepreneur

"I have bad games, but my confidence doesn't change."
~MARIANO RIVERA, MAJOR LEAGUE BASEBALL PLAYER

"If you want to be confident—be competent."
~PROFESSOR JOHN MCCARTHY, THE COACHES' COACH

"Anything you can pretend, you can master."
~MILTON ERICKSON, MD, MEDICAL HYPNOTIST

"I have often been afraid, but I would not give in to it. I made myself act as though I was not afraid, and, gradually, my fear disappeared."
~THEODORE ROOSEVELT, 26TH U.S. PRESIDENT

~Enthusiasm is contagious—start an epidemic.~

■ ■ ■

GO: 3-27-60-10

M***any of us want to go*** somewhere—maybe not necessarily a destination, but somewhere in our lives. Take that new job, acquire that higher-level skill, marry that perfect mate, go on that trip, etc. We *want* to do that thing, yet we often feel held back. Why? What is holding us back? Why don't we go for it?

Gilbert breaks us down into four groups—explorers, pioneers, settlers, and the nevers.

Group 1: The explorers. Only 3% of people fall into this category. These are the first to check out that "new thing." They march into the unknown, as William Shatner famously said on *Star Trek*, they "Go where no man has gone before." In the world we live in today, much of this is technology, new gadgets, electric cars, investments, etc. The explorers. The risk-takers.

Next are the *pioneers,* the first on the scene after the explorers. Twenty-seven percent of us fall into this group. They are still new, still not 100% certain about that "thing," the second group to be there.

The third group is most everyone: *the settlers, at 60%.* These are the believers after the fact, when everything has been established, when it is a sure thing. This is the majority of people, the masses.

Then, there is the last group: those who will **never** get on board, never buy in, and just *never* change. They refuse to move forward; they're just content to be stuck where they are, intentionally. The *nevers* are 10% of the people.

I can remember a time when I was the principal at Port Jervis Schools, and I wanted to hang college pennants in the café from each staff member who went to our school. I wanted the students to see where the adults went to school to get them thinking about college and their life after graduation. We named the café "University Hall."

Bam! There was a handful of people who had their pennant to me the next day, and I hung them immediately. Then, just like these percentage breakdowns, the rest started to come. A second wave of pennants came in a couple of weeks later. Then, after seeing the pennants up on the wall—and with me repeatedly asking and posting pictures of the pennants, etc.—a large group finally got me their pennants, and I got them up on the wall. University Hall was looking good!

I created a checklist of the staff and walked along, looking at the pennants and checking each person's name off the list of those who had turned it in. There were about ten or so staff members who hadn't given me their college pennant yet. I went and asked a few, sent some email reminders, and praised and thanked those who had participated.

Nope, I'm not going to get them. Some flat-out told me no, they didn't want to participate, and some offered the excuse, "Oh, I keep forgetting . . ." *The nevers. 10%*

I would not be stopped. I wanted this for our kids, so I called the schools of those colleges we didn't have yet, and asked the admissions office to send a pennant to our school so their college/university could be represented in our project. *Bam!* What do you think happened?

The schools sent them, and I hung them up! Don't let the *nevers* stop you on your journey.

Where are you on that journey? What category would you say you are in? Does it depend on the situation? This is a great reflection exercise for you to do during quiet reflection time.

When I wrote my first book, when I arrived at Guilford College and the basketball program not knowing anyone, and when I moved away from home—these were not *explorer* situations but definitely *pioneering* situations. I was the first in my immediate family and friend group to do these things, and they were new for me.

Here are four tips for you, no matter where you are on your journey or what group you are in (maybe *not* the *nevers*, because they wouldn't do them, anyway. The nevers probably aren't reading this book, either!)

1. Ask others who have done what you want to do, want to go, want to become. Be curious, and hear from those who have done it already.
2. Do your best, and forget the rest. Be focused and dedicated to what you are trying to achieve and become. Like Nike says, *Just do it,* and do the best you can.
3. Forgive yourself. If you miss a day, make a mistake, or take a step you don't love, forgive yourself. Admit it, fix it, and move on. Like a bird pooping on your windshield—spray and wipe, and keep going.
4. Just that: Keep going. I love Dr. Gilbert's saying, the mantra: *Don't quit, can't fail. Don't quit, can't fail.* It is so true. I got away from writing this book during a really busy time in my life, but something kept calling me back. I wanted to do it, but I just wasn't. So I made the important thing the important thing and got back to it. Each morning before work, every day, 45 minutes—and *Bam!* You are now reading the *Magic Acronyms* book. Just keep going. Keep rolling on your journey.

FROM THE SUCCESS HOTLINE ARCHIVES . . .

"No risk. No reward."
"No pain. No gain."

"No pressure. No diamonds."
~Mark Glicini, pro lacrosse player and sport psychology expert

"The cave you fear to enter holds the treasure you seek."
~Joseph Campbell, mythologist

"It's better to be a lion for a day than a sheep all your life."
~Sister Mary Kenny, Australian nurse

~The road to success is always under construction.~

■ ■ ■

MAKE 'EM THIRSTY

It is a pet peeve of mine when I hear folks complaining about motivation. People say things like, "They just won't listen, or they're not interested in learning." This *can* be true for some people. You might never get them, but you can reach most of them. I am challenging you to *shift your mindset.* Change your paradigm just a little—from *trying to motivate or move people forward* to *making them thirsty.* Make them thirsty to learn, grow, work, and do that ____ you are trying to make happen.

This comes from the saying, "You can lead a horse to water, but ______________. Fill in the blanks.

You've heard it. You know it. "You can lead a horse to water, but *you can't make 'em drink.*" Again, this may be true, but it doesn't have to be the reality. It doesn't have to be *your* reality. *Make the horse thirsty.* Set the conditions for the horse to drink that water on their own terms.

Well, what about people? We're *not* dealing with horses; we are dealing with *people*—people in schools, businesses, sports teams, unions, and more. How can this work here?

Let's sub out the word "thirsty" and put in ______. What word or strategy would you put in? What works for you? I like "curious." Make them *curious.* Maybe ask a question instead of telling them what to do. How would you do it? Remember: Mastery, autonomy, and purpose. (See Daniel Pink's *reasons for motivation* in the next excerpt.

Another word can be *passion.* When people can chase their passions in and outside of work, they are more energized and more "into it," as Dr. Gilbert would say. Find people's passion, and they will become alive. People are excited about the things they are passionate about.

Where there is a will, there is a way. Find that way. It might be as easy as asking the person, "What will make this task/job/assignment more meaningful for you?" If you don't know, this is pretty direct, and they will respect you more and hopefully work with more motivation because you asked. Keep rolling, friends.

FROM THE SUCCESS HOTLINE ARCHIVES . . .

Dr. Rob: "Passion persuades."
"No one works harder than a curious child."

"Don't ask yourself what the world needs. Ask yourself what makes you come alive, and go do that. Because what the world needs is people who have come alive!"

~Dr. Howard Thurman, philosopher

~ A setback is a setup for a comeback.~

~Willie Jolley~

■ ■ ■

MASTERY, AUTONOMY, AND PURPOSE

In addition to Dr. Gilbert and the Success Hotline, I am a big fan of Daniel Pink—his books, podcasts, TED talks, and more. In his TED talk "The Puzzle of Motivation," he shared the biggest motivator for people. It is *not* money, it is *not* power, it is *not* fame—three simple-yet-giant concepts. It will be extremely satisfying if you can achieve these goals in your own life. It is doubly gratifying if you can offer these three concepts to those you lead or those you work with.

Mastery, autonomy, and purpose. That's it. *These are the things that motivate people.* To do that thing well, in their own way, and with a meaningful purpose. Think about the work you are doing now. At times, it can be challenging to have any of these, but when you do, it is *the best.*

We've all heard the saying, "If you find a career that you love, you'll never work a day in your life!" These are the core ingredients to that statement: mastery, autonomy, and purpose. You might not have all three at once, either, and that's okay. If you have one, that's pretty good. Keep at it. Keep showing up and doing good work, and the others will follow.

You also may be asking, "I don't have these at work, but I would like them. How can I have them or get them?" *Do a great job! That* is the answer. Do amazing work, be an energizing and enthusiastic team member, do more than expected, etc., and good things will happen. When your work and performance exceed expectations, people see you in a different light. They see you doing other, greater things. Maybe different ideas pop into the supervisors' and the decision-makers' heads, and *Boom!* Who do they think of? *You!*

A friend of mine is a guidance counselor. She is amazing at her job: good with people, loves the kids, efficient, timely, etc. She is also exceptional at working with and talking with parents. Parents meet with the school staff, and they are stressed and sometimes aggressive. She is like the *parent-whisperer.* She calms them, listens to them, and helps direct and lead the conversation in a way that is a win-win for all.

District staff started to notice this and talk about it. "Wow, she is really good at working with parents." A conversation here, a proposal there, and *Bam!* She became the first-ever parent-coach in the district. They'd never even *had* that position before. It was because this counselor had gone above and beyond the job expectations and stood out working with parents; people saw her in a different light. She now works not only with parents but also with mastery, autonomy, and purpose!

FROM THE SUCCESS HOTLINE ARCHIVES . . .

Dr. Rob: Excellence is not *expected* effort.
Excellence is *extra effort.*

~Be a thermostat, not a thermometer.~

■ ■ ■

CHAPTER 4

IMPACT

"A life is not important unless it has a positive impact on others."

—Jackie Robinson

"If you're going to live, leave behind a legacy. Make an impact on the world that can never be erased."

—Maya Angelou

The Magic
ACRONYMS, FORMULAS, & IMPACTFUL STORIES
of Leadership

A Tribute to the Amazing Dr. Rob Gilbert *& the Success Hotline*

PMMFIT

by Ed Agresta

Ed Agresta is a teacher and coach from New Jersey who has been using GOYA both in the classroom and on the field. Ed has taught and coached for more than fifty years and authored multiple leadership and inspirational books. Agresta is a fascinating, humorous speaker and a gifted communicator who has given more than 1500 presentations to corporations, schools, and athletic teams.

Dr. Rob: Ed Agresta is America's greatest motivational speaker EVER!

▪

I ***first met Dr. Gilbert*** when I was on the football staff at Montclair State. He was playing Santa Claus for the families. The interesting part of this encounter was that he requested a picture and the name of the child who would be there. He did this so when the children came into the room and sat on his knee, they felt like Santa knew them and made them feel special.

The first question my daughter asked me was, "How did he know my name?" I knew at that moment that I had to get to know this gentleman. I saw how special he made these kids feel. I was curious how he did all this in such a short period of time. I realized he was not an ordinary college professor. He was a person who saw that, when you make a person feel important, you can go a long way in achieving things.

I discovered later that he would practice something I call *PMMFIT*, which stands for "Please Make Me Feel Important Today."

I utilize this as a teacher, coach, and parent. Dr. Gilbert does this with all his students and the people he mentors.

Dr. Rob mentored me for many years, taking me to some of his presentations, speaking in front of his classes, and going to organizations that had hired him to teach them the strategies for success. I became a better teacher, coach, and presenter by using the skills and strategies he taught me. He never asked for anything in return except that I just get better at what I was doing. He used to tell me that you have to be enthusiastic, have a clear message, have a strategy, feel comfortable being uncomfortable, be a good storyteller, and make the presentation memorable, whether you're in the classroom or in front of an organization. He instilled in me the strategy of GOYA. GOYA stands for "Get Off Your Anatomy." (Chapter 3)

We would meet almost every Sunday morning at the diner for breakfast or at his home. He would share new stories and any new magic tricks he'd learned. Dr. Gilbert would always hand me piles of tapes and books that would make me a better presenter and teacher.

The following week, I would bring them back, and he would have another set for me to use and go over. In fact, my family thought that I was a miniature Dr. Rob Gilbert. It was a great honor to be able to follow my mentor. After a while, I developed my own style of presentation, but I never forgot the basics that he taught me.

I also learned how to use magic and juggling to get people's attention during my classes and presentations. Full disclosure: I would not use the knives that Dr. Gilbert used when juggling. I was very happy with stuffed balls and socks. This was another way to engage the audience and teach a strategy that could be applied to their lives. I would follow up with the question, "How can you take the strategy and relate it to your life?" I would ask them to please share their thoughts with the class.

Action steps: In order to GOYA, you must force yourself to behave differently from how you feel. "State—Strategy—Content" are the keys to teaching or learning new material. You must be in a state to learn *and* have a strategy, before you can learn the content.

FROM THE SUCCESS HOTLINE ARCHIVES . . .

Dr. Rob: A veteran teacher said that it took her years to figure out that 2 > 4. This is especially true in the classroom. Even if you are teaching math! How can this be true? Teachers have to realize that, when they ask a question, listening *to* the student answering the question is more important than listening *for* the answer! To be honest, 2 is *not* greater than 4, but TO > FOR. Absolutely! Positively!! Guaranteed!!!

~You are not judged by the number of times you fail. You are judged by the number of times you succeed, and the number of times you succeed is directly related to the number of times you fail and keep on trying.~

■ ■ ■

SEE

D*r. Gilbert has talked about SEE often*—this acronym is connected to the work he does on the Hotline. He says it is one of the ultimate goals of an educator—and one who inspires. SEE. **S**ignificant **E**motional **E**xperiences. Create these for others. Move their spirits, and warm their souls. Create SEEs for them on their journey and in their lives.

In my whole life as an educator, I have tried to create SEEs for my students and staff, whether it was a field trip to the local zoo or science experiments in class.

How do we do it? When can we do it? Who do we do it for?

Let's start with how: You look for them—all the time. There are so many opportunities to do so. Nominate someone for an award. Send them a special congratulations, or surprise them with that really nice recognition. These things matter.

One of the first really nice SEEs I experienced as a Port Jervis School leader was from my Superintendent, John Xanthis. He nominated me for the Mid-Hudson Study Council Award for School Leadership. I was so thrilled. I was a new assistant principal and did not know what I was doing; I was just working as hard as possible. I was making progress in helping the school culture, but I was still not confident in what I was doing.

This award and this recognition from John Xanthis invigorated me—made me want to do more, be better. It had a significant impact on me and created a SEE—a *significant emotional experience*—for me and my family. My mom and wife came to the ceremony, and both were so proud of me—and I couldn't have been more proud to make them proud of me! *Wow!*

SEEs are contagious. From this experience early in my leadership career, I learned a few very important things. Doing these things for others created a lot of SEEs, which made me feel great about the work I was doing—*Recognition, Celebration, Acknowledgment, and more.*

- *Nominating others for awards. My team went on to nominate many others in Port Jervis for not only this regional award but for state and national awards, too. They matter.*
- Any chance I could, I tried to shine the spotlight on someone else—a speech, the announcements, a social media post, a ball game, etc. If I got a mic or camera, it was easy to find something kind and good to say and share about someone else. When you look for SEEs, you can find them—a lot. You know who else benefits from SEEs? Loved ones of that person that you create it for—kids, parents, relatives, friends—all are proud of that person creating a feel-good situation all the way around.
- Personal notes and pictures. After the ceremony was over for me, a week or so later, I got a letter in the mail from John X. It was an additional letter of congratulations from him along with the speech he wrote that day. *Wow.* I saved it and remember it fondly today.

All of these experiences from this event made me feel special. I learned quickly that, in my role as a school leader, I could provide

SEEs for others in many ways, such as attending weddings, award ceremonies, hospital visits, and more.

SEEs can be negative, too. All the recognitions and acknowledgments above are positive. Good vibes and good feelings. One thing that really sticks out to me was when my son lost a school election. He attends a school where we live, near Port Jervis.

He was pretty bummed, and I asked him more about it. I pressed further. There had to be some adult who could have given him some encouragement, could have given something to pep him up—like *Keep your chin up.* Nope. Nada. Not one adult said anything to him.

My wife and I were super-disappointed about this. This was a SEE for Matthew, our son—a SEE negative in nature that could have been helped by an adult connecting with him, making him feel better. Dr. Gilbert often shares the story of Abraham Lincoln losing many elections over his career. Winners lose more than losers lose. I wish someone had done this for my guy when he was down.

SEEs are everywhere for us. They don't have to be expensive or extravagant. They need to be timely, authentic, and intentional. Keep looking for them. They fill your bucket, the bucket of the person you do it for, and their family's bucket. SEEs are the real deal for you and those you serve. Dr. Gilbert has been delivering SEEs his whole life, especially for three minutes daily on the Hotline.

FROM THE SUCCESS HOTLINE ARCHIVES . . .

Dr. Rob: A rule that will *never* fail you: Catch people doing something right, and tell them about it. If you want to take this rule to the next level: Catch people doing something right, and celebrate it!

~Things always work out for me.~

~Dr. Terrie Wurzbacher~

■ ■ ■

TREES AND SHADE

You know that feeling when you hear or see something that shakes you immediately—that's what happened when I heard Hashim Garret say this when he visited Port Jervis Schools. Hashim is a former gangster from New Jersey, now a motivational speaker who has transformed his life. I respect him and the message he brings to schools around the country. He shared the old African saying: "He or she who plants the tree, rarely gets to enjoy the shade." I'll write it again—*he or she who plants the tree rarely gets to enjoy the shade.*

Think about the work you are doing, whether it is in schools, business, or something else. Are you making an impact? Will you see your impact—the positive impact you are having on others or that you *want* to have on others? Planting those seeds, planting those trees. I love this quote I heard from Hashim. It makes you think—you may not see the impact or the growth, but you have to know and believe that you will make a difference. Think about Dr. Martin Luther King, Jr. Did he see what his impact was? Did he get to enjoy the shade? No. Abraham Lincoln? No.

Now, think about painting. I have always found something relaxing about painting a house or room. The color is going smoothly onto the flat surface and changing what it was. You can work for one hour, step back, and totally see the change, the difference you made.

This quote, this mindset, is the total opposite. You are *doing* for others, yet you may not see the benefits right away. I am so grateful for this photo below.

This is in the spring of my twentieth year at Port Jervis Schools. I received this pink dogwood tree in my first few years at Port Jervis from Home Depot as a donation. I asked for it to help the campus look beautiful. I was looking to do anything I could to make Port the best it could be. I planted it that spring and then waited. Waited and waited. No flowers. For years, no flowers. I was strongly urged to remove it because I was told it was dead and an eyesore. I pleaded, "No, let's give it some more time." I raked and irrigated around it, gave it some fertilizer, and waited some more. Yes—eventually, years later, it started to bloom.

This picture was taken more than ten years after I planted the tree, and *I do* get to enjoy its shade. I do get to see its beauty and know that others in Port Jervis enjoy it, too. I see it daily, and it reminds me of the important work I am doing and that there is more to be done. I may not see the results right away or feel the impact of my efforts, yet I know it is important to keep planting, keep working.

FROM THE SUCCESS HOTLINE ARCHIVES . . .

Dr. Rob: One day, when Grandpa was in his garden, his four-year-old grandson asked him why he loved to be in his garden so much.

Grandpa said, "I love it because my garden teaches me so many life lessons."

"Tell me one," the grandson asked.

"Good things take time," said the grandfather. "My garden has taught me how to have patience."

"Wow," said the four-year-old, with excitement, "I can't wait until I have patience."

~There are three types of people: Those who make it happen, those who watch things happen, and those who wonder what happened.~

■ ■ ■

BE THE COFFEE BEAN

Books can be incredibly impactful. Dr. Gilbert recommends them all the time on the Hotline. You can read something, absorb it, see it in your mind, and then become what you have read. It is true magic when that happens. While I struggled to become a reader early in life, I became a reader as an adult. I knew I could always find a nugget or gem of improvement and growth—or get lost in another John Grisham thriller. Fun fact: I've read/listened to all of his books!

The Coffee Bean, by John Gordon and Damon West, is a great book. I was *into* the story immediately and could identify with every part of it. Without giving the story away completely, Damon shares a story from when he was in prison; a veteran inmate talked to him about how to survive in prison, how to navigate all the challenges of the different groups and gangs, and more.

The inmate described to Damon that prison can be like a boiling pot of water in many ways. As an inmate, you were in that boiling water, so who did you want to be: a carrot, an egg, or a coffee bean?

- *The carrot.* What happens to carrots in boiling water? They get mushy and soft, lose their nutrients, wilt, and lose their firmness.
- *The egg.* It becomes brittle and hard. The shell loses its strength and becomes porous. The egg becomes a lot less desirable than a normal egg.

- *Lastly, the coffee bean.* What does that do? How does it respond to boiling water? When coffee beans are combined with boiling water, they change the whole environment. They make that water go from something that was quite dangerous—burning everyone—to something most everyone loves. People want it daily and grow to love a wonderful cup of hot, delicious coffee.

It really is a great story. Kudos to Gordon and West for collaborating on such a great project. They've written a second edition, *How to Be a Coffee Bean* and also a coffee-bean book for kids. While many of us can't identify with being in prison, we can relate to challenging situations and dealing with difficulty. How do some people just rise above the pettiness and the fighting? How do some folks just be that special person who others want to be around and just seem happy and joyful even in difficult times? *They are coffee beans.* They change the whole environment for the better. They are thoughtful and intentional, looking to support, and have a positive impact in the lives of others—and more.

There are many ways to be a coffee bean. Pause for a moment, and put this book down. On paper or on your phone, write down ten ways you can be a coffee bean in a challenging situation in your life. It could be work, family, or the project you're working on that has stalled. How can you be a coffee bean and change the environment for the better?

I hope you found that exercise helpful. You don't need magic or training to be a coffee bean. You just have to be intentional, creative, and thoughtful on your journey, working and interacting with others in good times and bad. Be a coffee bean!

FROM THE SUCCESS HOTLINE ARCHIVES . . .

Dr. Rob: "Of all the virtues we can learn, no trait is more useful, more essential for survival, and more likely to improve the quality of our life than the ability to transform adversity into an enjoyable challenge."

~Mihaly Csikszentmihalyi, psychologist

~Are you going to say, "I'm glad I did" or "I wish I would have"?~

■ ■ ■

UNLESS

"**U***nless.*"

It is not an acronym. I use this word and concept from a different doctor. He, too, is a great storyteller and has impacted many by his words and actions. It is the last line from the book, *The Lorax*, by the great author Dr. Seuss. "***Unless** someone like you cares a whole awful lot, nothing will ever get better. It's not.*" I love this book. I love this line, and I love reading it each year to kids in schools during Dr. Seuss Day.

Think about it. It makes you think about yourself and the impact you can have with your family and at work, in school, and in the community. It puts it right back on you: If you're not gonna do it, who is? If you're not gonna pick up that piece of paper, who will? If you're not gonna display kindness, who will?

Unless. I also like it because it's a challenge. Through the wonderful story of the Lorax, Dr. Seuss challenges kids and adults to do more, similar to Dr. Gilbert's concept of "Do more than expected." He is asking us to be the one who will make the world a better place in a way that is non-threatening but makes us think.

It also provides hope. In the story of the Lorax, Dr. Seuss goes on to give the young boy in the story a seed. The boy is to plant and grow the seed of the last truffula tree. Nurture it, take care of it, and support it to replenish the destroyed population of the truffula trees. Hope. "Unless" provides hope for our future, and I hope you will, too! Thank you for caring. You are that person!

FROM THE SUCCESS HOTLINE ARCHIVES . . .

The World's Greatest Teammate

Dr. Rob: Bianca loved basketball. She played in a church league in central New Jersey. Early in the season, one of her teammates missed practice. Two days later, Bianca called the girl and offered to come over to show her what she missed.

A simple call. A simple act of caring. Bianca gets it. In case you don't . . .

When was the last time you missed school or practice or work and someone called you and offered to come over and help you? More importantly, when was the last time you called someone, like Bianca did? Bianca cared, but she also *showed* that she cared.

Thanks, Bianca!

Oh, by the way: When this story took place, Bianca was in only the third grade! (I want to thank the great Coach Darren Ventre for telling me this story!)

~Life is a marathon, not a sprint.~

■ ■ ■

SIMPLIFIERS OR COMPLICATORS

I *learned this great concept* from my ACC (Atlantic Coast Conference) men's college basketball officiating supervisor, John Clougherty. Regardless of your work, do you want to be a simplifier or a complicator? Do you make things simpler for your team or more difficult? Do you gum things up or make them run more smoothly?

In the world of basketball officiating, this meant making the correct calls at the right moment. Getting the plays right that were right in front of you. Answer questions when asked, and be in the right place and at the right time, doing the right thing (that is a Dr. Gilbert-ism from longtime and Hall of Fame Montclair State University Men's Basketball Coach Ollie Gelston).

So, what could it mean for you in your role as a leader or educator? Here are a few ideas:

- **Be on time:** Very simple. Control the controllable. We've heard many leaders say: "'On time' is fifteen minutes early."
- **Ask:** How can I help, or what can I do to contribute? Be a do-er. Show up and help.
- **Be a connector:** Connect people, resources, ideas, and solutions. You might not know how to do it, but maybe you know someone who does.
- **Be kind, show class, and respect:** When you work, act, and go about your business with these intentional actions and

behaviors, you cannot go wrong. You will be well-received by others and just naturally be a simplifier.

- **Be mindful:** Be mindful of others' space, culture, gender, upbringing, stresses, goals, and more. Example: You work in a busy, large school. Do you know what the superintendent's or principal's goals are? Are you helping carry the banner and supporting them, the school, and the district by your actions and behaviors?

Be a simplifier, not a complicator.

FROM THE SUCCESS HOTLINE ARCHIVES . . .

Which one are you?
There are only two types of people in the world:
#1. Those who do.
#2. Those who don't.
The difference between them:
#1. Those who do—*do.*
#2. Those who don't—*don't.*
Are you a "doer" or a "don'ter"?
Doers say,
"I'll do it whether I feel like it or not."
Don't-ers say, "I'll do it when I feel like it."
For doers: Their commitments are stronger
than their feelings.
For don't-ers:
Their feelings are stronger than their commitments.
When your diet is more important than that cookie . . .

Working out is more important than hanging out . . .
Then your commitments are stronger than your feelings.
Doers get results. Don't-ers have reasons why they didn't get results.
Is it easy to be a *doer*? No.
Is it doable? Yes!

~Play like a champion today.~

▪ ▪ ▪

MTC

This is not a Dr. Gilbert story but an Andrew Marotta story. It is a real, personal story that means the world to me. I truly believe that things happen for a reason and that good things come to good people. I am blessed to have married my wife, my high school sweetheart, on April 21, 2001. In my ring, she wrote: **MTC.** "MTC" stands for "My True Companion," the love song written by Marc Cohn in 1991. This was our song growing up together, courting together, and falling in love with one another. I loved it, and I cherish my relationship with my wife and the ring itself.

Fast-forward twelve years. I am painting a shoe cubby in our garage for our three children. I asked Claire, the oldest, which cubby she wanted. She pointed to the square on the right. Matthew, our son, the second oldest, pointed to the one on the left. Tess, the baby, didn't really have a choice and got the one in the middle. I began painting their first initial in each box, going left to right. As I began to sketch out the "T" in the middle of the cubby, my mouth dropped, my heart sank, and I said out loud: "M-T-C!" I yelled to my wife to come quickly. She saw what I saw: MTC, and we both began to cry. We did *not* name the kids with those initials to match my ring, yet the letters played out. It was a beautiful moment.

We had been discussing getting couples tattoos. When we discovered MTC at that moment, we knew right away that MTC was the tattoo. Not only was it our love for each other, but it also represented our children. I loved it!

Fast forward again. 2019. We bought a small beach home in Miramar Beach, Florida. Miramar Beach is located in the beautiful panhandle area of northern Florida. It is a small, cute place in a lovely little neighborhood. We sat around one evening throwing names out to name the place. *Miramar Beach:* It is very tropical there; the place is a cute little house . . . Miramar, Miramar Tropical . . . *Miramar Tropical Cabana!* MTC again! The joy and excitement grew once again.

I share this story of MTC to challenge you to think. *What are the most important things in your life?* And do they match up in some way? Is there some connection that can be a slogan, a mindset, and a motto for you and your family, your life? I look at the MTC tattoo on my arm and the letters in my ring. They mean so much to me, and I love how they lined up—without even planning it. Brainstorm with your team, and see if there are some pieces, parts, people, letters, etc., that line up with your core values, your beliefs. Maybe they can turn into an MTC for you and your team.

FROM THE SUCCESS HOTLINE ARCHIVES . . .

Dr. Rob: "The most important thing is to make the most important thing the most important thing. Don't major in minor things."

"The moment you commit and quit holding back, all sorts of unforeseen incidents, meetings, and material assistance will rise up to help you. The simple act of commitment is a powerful magnet for help."
~NAPOLEON HILL, AUTHOR

Harmon Killebrew, baseball Hall of Famer, told the story about how his father used to play with his brother and him in the front yard.

His mother would come out and say, "You're tearing up the grass."

His dad would reply, "We're not raising grass—we're raising boys."

~The most important thing is to make the most important thing the most important thing. That's the most important thing!~

■ ■ ■

PURE FRIENDSHIP

by Doug Cooney

Doug Cooney is President of Deerfield Associates, a nationally known and retained executive-search firm that focuses on senior-level search work in the education sector. Doug is also a former national TV sportscaster, including on-air assignments with NBC sports, trips to China (with Bob Costas), the 1988 Summer Olympics held in Seoul, South Korea, and broadcasting work with ESPN and TBS (The Goodwill Games). Doug attributes much of his success both as a professional headhunter of talent and on-air TV broadcaster to his trusted and talented best friend, Rob Gilbert! You can learn more at deerfieldassociates.com

▪

R***ob Gilbert is a legend!*** More importantly, he is a best friend forever.

Rob and I first met in the mid-1970s, when we both worked at UMass Amherst for the orientation program for new students. We also both served at UMass as head of residences in student housing in the Southwest Towers. I was located on the 12th floor, Rob was on the 19th floor, and we each were responsible for 200 students in our respective dormitories—not easy to do at such lofty heights.

Rob and I were roommates at the 1976 summer Olympics held in Montreal, Canada.

When I later aspired to be a national television sports announcer for ESPN, Turner Broadcasting (TBS Goodwill Games), and NBC Sports, it was Rob who believed in me right from the start.

When I later served as on-air announcer and host at the 1988 Olympics for NBC TV Sports coverage from Seoul, South Korea, Rob taped all 180 hours of coverage. Upon my return from Seoul, Rob gave me a box full of VHS tapes which included every minute of NBC's coverage! That is *pure friendship* at its best.

We have been great friends, sharing many adventures and life experiences both personally and professionally.

Rob cares enormously for his students at Montclair State College/ University, and he continues to be passionate about teaching and inspiring his students to new heights.

Rob's personal interest in connecting people and purpose is most evident in his remarkable venture "Success Hotline." Rob was recently featured in an exclusive story on this accomplishment in the UMass Amherst alumni magazine. Well done, Rob!

I can call Rob anytime, including 5:30 a.m., and he always answers and always has the best advice. Rob Gilbert has more "common sense" than anyone I know. But, it always comes back for me to being grateful for having such a best friend.

FROM THE SUCCESS HOTLINE ARCHIVES . . .

Dr. Rob: A British publication once offered a prize for the best definition of a "friend."

Among the thousands of answers were the following:

"One who multiplies joy, divides grief, and whose honesty is inviolable."

"One who understands our silence."

"A watch that beats true for all time and never runs down."

The winning definition was: "A friend is the one who comes in when the whole world has gone out."

~There is nothing on this earth to be prized more than true friendship.~

~Thomas Aquinas

▪ ▪ ▪

CHAPTER 5

STRATEGIES

"Life is not a talent game. ***It is a strategy game.*** *Find the right strategy, and you can do anything."*

~Coach Mike Tully

The Magic

ACRONYMS, FORMULAS, & IMPACTFUL STORIES

of Leadership

A Tribute to the Amazing Dr. Rob Gilbert *& the Success Hotline*

FFF

D*r. Gilbert, throughout his time* running the Hotline, is always giving us a roadmap to be successful, to be impactful, and to help us reach our goals. We have to do the work, yet he has shown us the way. Here is another one of those: *The 3 Fs.* These Fs sound like they could be a bad word, but they are not. They are magic words; they are a recipe for success: find, find out, and follow.

1. Find: *Find that person* in your life who is doing what you want to do or is who you want to become. Is it a famous person, a teacher you had, an author you read, or an athlete you competed against? Pick multiple successful people in the area you are interested in, and write them down.
2. Find out: *Find out their strategies!* Find out what it is that they do that makes them successful, impactful, and more. Dr. Gilbert has said countless times: "Life is *not* a talent game. Life is a strategy game, and when you find the right strategy, you can do anything."

   One personal example is writing. I fell in love with writing—books, my blogs, etc. I write often, but how could I become a better writer, the best writer? I read *The Miracle Morning for Writers*, by Hal Elrod. I learned a lot from that book, but the biggest strategy was that most writers write early and every day. *Early and every day.* Yes! These were great tips, and here I am right now—writing Dr. Gilbert's book at 7:30 a.m. on a Sunday morning in a quiet space.

Another goal I had on my writing journey was to increase my 5-star reviews on Amazon. They are there, but just not in the quantity I would have hoped. Then, I interviewed Honoree Corder on my #ELB Podcast. I met Honoree, of course, at a Dr. Gilbert Zoom seminar!

You can view the #ELB podcast with Honoree here: https://bit.ly/ELBpodcastHonoree

In preparing for the podcast, I watched Honoree's TED Talk called *Authenticity Is the New Black*; you can find it with an easy YouTube search. Incredibly, she shared the same topic during her talk, at the 6:45 minute mark about: increasing her 5-star reviews. What happened next was just amazing. She decided that, for any great book she read, she would write a 5-star review. If she wanted 5-star reviews, she *would write them* for others. She had to model the behavior and actions she wanted to see in others. Honoree then left Hal Elrod a 5-star review for his book *The Miracle Morning.* Well, the very next day . . .

I'll leave the second half of Honoree's story for you to watch in the TED Talk, but what happened was just perfect and really reaffirms what Dr. Gilbert says about the 3 Fs: Find, find out, and now number three:

3. Follow: I, too, have now adopted this practice of writing 5-star reviews. If it is something that I want in my life, then I need to do it for others. I am following this advice from Honoree and putting it into practice. Find, find out, and follow. Follow what that person is doing, and good things will happen to you, too. Maybe it won't happen in the exact way it did for them, but good things will happen.

It seems so simple, right? *Find, find out, and follow.* Why don't we do more of this? Why haven't we started this earlier? I think this is excellent advice from the legendary Dr. Gilbert, and I am thrilled to put it into practice in my own life.

FROM THE SUCCESS HOTLINE ARCHIVES . . .

Dr. Rob: No matter what you want to achieve, *The Four Steps to Success* will serve as a great roadmap!

#1. Know where you are.
#2. Know where you want to get to.
#3. Figure out how to get from Step #1 to Step #2.
#4. *Do It!!!*

~When you help a teammate up the hill,
you find yourself closer to the top.~
~Irv Furman, professional speaker and magician~

■ ■ ■

ALL IN

D*r. Gilbert asks this question often* on the Hotline: "Are you going to go *all in*, or are you going to hold back?" He says this is the only thing you need to know about sports psychology. Of course, if you want something, you are going to say, *all in!* Who wouldn't?

I'm sure many of you reading and listening to this book are professionals who have busy and rich lives. It is hard to go *all in* on one thing—but it is that one thing that is the key. It is that one thing that you want to be great at, right? What about your family? Your church? Your other responsibilities?

As I write this excerpt, we just finished a family weekend of skiing in the Berkshires of Massachusetts. I stayed behind at the resort, and my family left midday Sunday afternoon. I am now going to write this evening and half the day tomorrow to be back in time to attend my son's game. See? I'm *all in* on my writing and surviving-and-thriving speaking career, yet I'm *all in* on my family first. How can I be *all in* on more than one thing? My school, my fitness, my financial security, and more?

I think finding what that ____ (person, action, focus, job, thing, etc.) you want to be *all in* on is the key. If you neglect your loved ones, your job, or your health, things are going to be challenging for you. If you can find the right blend and harmony of *all in* in your life, I think that is the magic sauce.

It came to me in the spring of 2023—that *all in* moment. My kids were teenagers, my wife and I had been married 20+ years, and I'd been at my job in Port Jervis Schools for 20 years. I had stability, longevity, purpose, and more. The writing and inspirational speaking continued to pull at me. I wanted to make more of an impact and a greater connection with others.

Bam! It came to me. I found the perfect blend of family, focus, and passion. I shared the story of the very important tattoo I got, combining my family with my AM Surviving and Thriving logo. I was *all in* on these—my family and the work I am doing as a motivational author and speaker. To symbolize the *all in* and make it the most real it could be, I got it tattooed on my arm—I could see it, feel it, and visualize each day what was most important. It was a bold moment for me, a kind of "no-turning-back" moment, to me, which is *all in* to the extreme.

Back to the skiing weekend—this was the perfect combination of it all—family time, health and fitness, making memories, yet also including the *deep-work* time and *alone* time to finish this book while making it back in time for Matthew's basketball game the next day.

I look at many successful people who have lost what was most important to them chasing the *all in*. I think knowing what is most important and keeping your priorities in order while being immersed in the *all in* can be done. I know I am trying my hardest right now, and it is never easy and never perfect—surviving and thriving through it all, being ***all in!***

ARE YOU GOING TO BE "IN IT" OR "INTO IT"?

Are you going to be *In It* or *Into It*?
Are you going to *have a child* or *be a mom or a dad*?
Are you going to *go to school* or *be a student*?
Are you going to *play tennis* or *be a tennis player*?
Are you going to *be in a play* or *be an actor*?
Are you going to *play an instrument* or *be a musician*?
Are you going to *be married* or *be a husband or wife*?
Are you going to *just hear* or *really listen*?
Are you going to *play a sport* or *be an athlete*?
Are you going to *give a talk* or *be a speaker*?
Are you going to *cook* or *be a chef*?
Are you going to *plant flowers* or *be a gardener*?
Are you going to *write* or *be a writer*?
Are you going to *sell things* or *be a salesperson*?
Are you going to be an *order taker* or an *order getter*?
Are you going to *have a job* or *have a career*?
Are you going to *curse the darkness* or *light a candle*?
Are you going to *make promises* or *keep commitments*?
Are you going to *try* or *do*?
Are you going to *hold back* or *go all out*?
Are you going to *count the days* or *make the days count*?
Are you going to be a *spectator* or a *participant*?
Are you going to *set your limits* or *stretch your limits*?
Are you going to be *In It* or *Into It*?

Here's the one most important question . . .

Are you going to *just live*, or are you going to *be truly alive*?

~Are you going to go all in or hold back?~

~Dr. Rob Gilbert

▪ ▪ ▪

THE 15-MINUTE RULE

by Dr. John Delate

Dr. John Delate has served as an administrator and educator in higher education for more than 30 years. While overseeing the residence-life program at Montclair State University, he had the great fortune to co-teach freshmen seminar courses with Dr. Rob Gilbert. He is a great friend and colleague of Dr. Rob.

▪

I ***served as the Executive Director*** of Residence Life at Montclair State University for 4.5 years. During that span, I had the great fortune to co-teach a number of freshman seminars with Dr. Rob Gilbert. I should clarify the term "co-teach," as I learned much more from Dr. Gilbert and the students than I ever taught. It was an amazing experience to observe Dr. Gilbert provide a variety of stories to convey valuable information and great lessons. Each class was an adventure, and we all enjoyed the ride.

One recommendation for student success that Dr. Gilbert shared struck a deep chord with me. Dr. Gilbert noted that our actions lead and emotions follow, rather than the reverse, which many of us tend to believe. Dr. Gilbert applied this principle with a guide he called the *15-Minute Rule*. In essence, the rule stated that if one did not feel like doing some activity, such as going to the gym or completing homework, the person needed to just commit to starting the assignment and work on it for 15 minutes. At that point, the rule held that momentum would take over and that the action would continue for a longer period. One would now "feel" like continuing the work at hand.

I had struggled for years to complete my dissertation. Being a full-time employee as well as a husband and father, I rarely had the energy to write any part of the dissertation after hours. After hearing Dr. Gilbert's advocacy for the 15-Minute Rule, I decided to follow the guidelines. Each time I committed to working for only 15 minutes on the paper, I found myself going to 30, 45, 60, and more minutes. Even at times when I felt no energy to even start writing, I listened to Dr. Gilbert's voice and began the 15-minute practice. The results were amazing.

Within several months of following the rule, I had written more on the dissertation than I had the entire previous year. I continued the practice until I had completed writing my entire dissertation. It was nothing short of a miracle.

As Dr. Gilbert has reminded us over the years, life is not a game of talent; it is a game of strategy. The 15-Minute Rule is one such strategy that can produce incredible results. Believe me, I know.

FROM THE SUCCESS HOTLINE ARCHIVES . . .

Dr. Rob: Dr. Delate is the finest college administrator I have ever met. By the time he's reading this book, he will be a college or university president!!!

This is Dr. Delate's favorite Success Hotline story . . .

THE DIFFERENCE THAT MAKES THE DIFFERENCE

The late, great British actor Charles Laughton was attending a Christmas dinner at the home of a very wealthy British nobleman.

Just before they served dessert, the nobleman told everyone about their family ritual, in which each person tells a story, reads a favorite passage, or sings a song that reminds them of Christmas.

When it was Mr. Laughton's turn, he, in his magnificently trained voice, recited "The 23rd Psalm."

"The Lord is my Shepherd, I shall not want . . . ."

When he finished, everyone applauded.

When everyone was finished, the host realized that Auntie, who was 93, had fallen asleep in the next room over. Knowing how much she enjoyed this, he woke her up. When Auntie returned to the table, she, too, as she did every year, recited the "The 23rd Psalm."

"The Lord is my Shepherd, I shall not want . . . ."

When she finished, everyone cried.

When it was time for Mr. Laughton to leave, the nobleman asked him why people applauded when he recited the Psalm and cried when Auntie spoke the exact same Psalm.

Mr. Laughton responded, "It might have been the same Psalm, but there was a big difference. You see, I know the Psalm, but your Auntie knows the Shepherd!"

~You are stronger than your fears and better than your failures.~

■ ■ ■

EB + ED = BL

I *am active on social media* as a professional. I'm not posting blooper videos or telling you what I ate for dinner, but rather focusing on learning, growing, and sharing. One of my friends, whom I follow, admire, and have learned from, is Asael Ruvalcaba, from Brownsville, Texas. Asael is a veteran school leader who is active in his school, with his beautiful family and lovely wife, Amy, and with his health and wellness. He has written in several of my books and was even a guest on the #ELB podcast. You can watch/listen here: https://bit.ly/ELBAsaelRuvalcaba

Asael is a "fit" leader who works out every morning. He posts motivational pictures and quotes with his famous key line: "Send it!" I love "Send it." You can add so many things to that—it's short, simple, and inspiring.

One of the things Asael posted was "EB + ED = BL." *Eat better* plus *exercise daily,* equals a *better life.* Awesome, right? I love it. So true, yet how many of us don't do this? I am 49 years old, and, as I write this book, I am counting calories for the first time in my life. Asael's formula for a better life is more meaningful to me now than ever.

Last year, I slipped on ice and fell, breaking four ribs. At a recent doctor's visit, I had gained 12 pounds since last year. Yikes! I am feeling that 12 pounds everywhere, which brings me back to EB + ED = BL. I wanted an exceptional life for my next 50, so I had to act ***now*** on this. I have always eaten pretty well and certainly was very active in my younger years—as a dad, principal, former college basketball player, and former college basketball official. I was running four to five miles every night at my games.

That all stopped when I stepped away from officiating. Between the broken ribs and a lack of discipline with my eating and exercise routine, I fell off the wellness track and added on the pounds. Thank you, Asael, for bringing me back.

I now *live* the "EB + ED = BL." It is on my mind constantly, and I put steps into action to make it happen. I now:

- *Count my calories daily: 2100 in total.*
- *Work out every day from 5:30 a.m. to 6 a.m.*
- *Walk between a mile and two miles daily. At lunchtime, before my kids' games, before a school event, I power-walk the halls after school, etc. I make time to do it and get it done.*
- *Focus on the types of food I eat: low-calorie, high-protein, water, etc. Be intentional about it.*
- *Act on the inspiration that Asael and others provide.*
- *Continually work toward that BL: Better Life.*

I am grateful you are reading this book and encourage you to EB + ED for a BL. Thanks, Asael.

FROM THE SUCCESS HOTLINE ARCHIVES . . .

Dr. Rob: Want to live longer? Want to improve your longevity? Current research shows that there are five simple things you can do to live 13 to 16 years longer. Here are The Big Five:

1. Do not smoke.
2. Do not drink. If you must drink, drink no more than one drink a day for women and no more than two drinks a day for men. But, of course, it's best not to drink at all.
3. Moderate exercise. Marathon runners rarely live to be 100. Moderation is the key when it comes to exercise.
4. Eat mostly a plant-based diet. You don't have to become a vegan or a vegetarian, but you do have to increase fruits and veggies and cut down on meat intake.
5. Get your body weight down to where it should be, and keep it there for the rest of your life.

Remember when I said that these are five *simple* things? They are "simple," but they might not be easy. The Big Five are "simple" to understand, but they might not be so "easy" to do!

~The only time you run out of chances is
when you stop using them.~
~Patti LaBelle, singer~

■ ■ ■

THE 5 A.M. CLUB

T*hroughout this book*, I've sprinkled ideas, strategies, and formulas that are *not* from the Success Hotline, but they surely go along with Dr. Gilbert's message about being successful and being significant. This is another one: *The 5 a.m. Club*. I read this book, written by Robin Sharma, in the summer of 2020 on the shore of Lake Champlain, Vermont. Each day as I read, I began to get up earlier and earlier because I was so "*into*" the book and its message. Yes, that is the message: get up early to accomplish the things you want to in your life. It does sound simple, right? Then, why wasn't I doing it as often as I wanted?

The book made me reflect on what I really wanted in my life and the person I really wanted to be. The book tells a story about people going through a transformation in their lives that starts . . . yes, you guessed it, at 5 a.m. So, it is not a "how-to" book, but rather a story about how these people made these changes in their lives, all beginning with creating the quiet time in the morning.

How can this work for you? I've heard all the reasons why *not* to do this: I'm tired, I don't have time, I'm not a morning person, my family setup right now is not good, the kids are still young, I don't have space, I have to get ready for work. I've heard it all.

In this book, there are many strategies shared about starting something new that may be a challenge: "It's the start that stops most people, the 15-Minute rule, airtight compartments, C > F = R, and more. Here are some recommendations for getting started if you are curious about the 5 a.m. Club:

- *Get the book* The 5 a.m. Club, *and read it. It is also on Audible.*
- *Start trimming your bedtime back three minutes a night. To get up at 5 a.m. and feel good, you have to get the proper rest. Everyone's need for sleep is a little different, so get to that right time.*
- *Move your alarm clock/phone away from your bed. You are less likely to hit snooze if you move your clock away from your bed and have to actually get up and out of bed to turn it off.*
- *Clear your mornings—get any hurdles out of the way so you can start your day the way you want: make the coffee the night before, put out your exercise clothes right there in front of you, get the supplies or materials you need ready to go, etc.*
- *Make a list of what it is you want to accomplish during this magical, spiritual time, and keep it close to your workstation.*
- *Get the lighting, temperature, sounds, etc. all the way you want them to really enjoy the time.*
- *Do it daily, and get into the routine. Dr. Gilbert says that habits start out like small, thin threads, woven together over and over until they make a strong, thick cable.*
- *Start!*

There are no trophies, no awards, no recognition for you for joining the 5 a.m. Club, but there is an amazing satisfaction and fulfilling accomplishment of the things you really want to do in life. At 5 a.m., you get the time that so many of us desire. I challenge you to make it happen. It is 5:46 a.m. right now as I write this excerpt. It has been a goal of mine to make this book happen, and it is happening during the magical 5 a.m. time. Go for it!

FROM THE SUCCESS HOTLINE ARCHIVES . . .

Dr. Rob: Five thoughts on habits:

1. Human beings are habit-taking-on machines. Successful people have great habits.
2. "We become what we repeatedly do. Therefore, excellence is not an act, but a habit." ~Aristotle
3. If it's easy to do, it's also easy *not* to do.
4. "Make a commitment. Make it public. Make it happen." ~Frank Somma, sales trainer and author
5. Especially for students:

Poor study habits turn into poor grades.
Good study habits turn into good grades.
Great study habits turn into great grades.

Dr. William James, the father of American psychology, developed three steps for how to start a good habit:

Start immediately.
Do it flamboyantly.
No exceptions.

~The secret to getting ahead is getting started.~

■ ■ ■

SAVERS

I ***reference several books in this book*** that had a deep impact on me. This is one of them: *The Miracle Morning*, by Hal Elrod. I loved it. I dove right in, head first. There were many takeaways in the book that I implemented immediately: moving my alarm clock, prepping my clothes the night before, and SAVERS. SAVERS—yes. *Silence—**Affirmations**—**Visualization**—**Exercise**—**Reading**—Scribing.*

In the book, Hal declares that, if you do these six things each morning, you will set your day off on the right path. Who doesn't want that? I wanted that, and where I was in my life at the time, I was swamped. Three kids, 12 and younger. Busy professional life, all the while trying to survive and thrive. Let's break them down.

Silence: I am an extrovert. I am a captain in the extroverted world. I love people, exciting events, and cool happenings. I want to be there and in the heat of the excitement—yet I crave silence in my world. No radio, nothing in the car, no outside distractions, etc. Sit for five minutes or less each morning, with nothing happening. I do like coffee during this time. Let the thoughts flow and your heart beat.

Affirmations: Tell yourself you can do it. Tell yourself you can make it happen. If you aren't talking to yourself, then start. This book is filled with many affirmations from the great Dr. Rob!

Direct those thoughts and the things you want in your life. Who do you want to be? Tell yourself that you can be that person. Try this: Hold up your right hand. Touch your pointer finger, the first finger after your thumb, and say the word "I," *out loud.* Next, touch your middle finger to your thumb and say out loud, "can." Next, the ring finger, and then the pinky and say "do"; then say "this." *I-can-do-this.* Tell yourself that you can do it, believe you can do it, and then go do it! You got this!

Visualizations: Now visualize what it is you want to do—a presentation, a meeting, a performance. Visualize yourself being the person you know you can be. See yourself speaking, acting, and being energized and positive, shining through "all the stuff" that one has got going on. When you see yourself being successful, you take some steps to being successful in whatever it is you are trying to do. Life is challenging on its own. Add this to your toolbox, and you are on your way to being successful.

Exercise: Not too much explaining here. Like Nike has told us for years: *Just do it.* Your exercise doesn't have to be at a high-end, expensive gym or involve the most costly equipment. Just exercise. Just do it. Every day. Waking up and doing it right away is the best recipe. If you have to eat two frogs, eat the bigger one first!

A couple of tips to wake up early and get that exercise in: #1. Keep it simple. Have the shoes and clothes ready. Same place and easy to put on. #2. Same time: Go to bed at the same time, and wake up at the same time. We are creatures of habit. When we build these habits, they start out as thin threads and then build into thick cords. #3: Vices: It's hard to exercise when we give in to our vices too much—drinking, staying up late, smoking/vaping, not eating healthfully, etc. No lectures here—just limits. Cut out some of the vices that set you back the most. Trust my experience: You will feel better when you do; you'll be able to exercise with more energy and passion.

Reading and Scribing: I combined these last two. They go hand in hand. Some people can go old school and just straight-up read and write. They take the time to do those two things. Yes. You can. There's nothing like a paper book and a journal. I do mine a little bit differently. I do my reading each night. Fifteen minutes. Every night.

Yet, in the morning, I usually listen to an audio book or podcast, or read a short blog—something that is maybe a couple of minutes. For me, I scribe many times—I "talk-to-text" while I'm on the elliptical or while walking after a run. I write many of my leadership blogs that way (plug for the #ELB Education Leadership & Beyond blog. Sign up at andrewmarotta.com). I use the Google doc app, open a new doc, and talk to text. It is about 80% correct, it saves to my hard drive (happens automatically), and then I go back and clean it up at a different time. It helps me capture ideas.

I highly recommend *The Miracle Morning* and implementing SAVERS into your morning routine.

FROM THE SUCCESS HOTLINE ARCHIVES . . .

Dr. Rob: CHANGE IS NOT DIFFICULT.

Everyone knows how difficult it is to change. But everyone is *wrong*! Change is easy. Many smokers have stopped smoking hundreds of times. Many dieters have lost a ton of weight on diets. But smokers return to smoking, and dieters go off their diets. Change is easy. ***Keeping the change is hard.***

It's easy to stop smoking. It's hard to *stay stopped*. It's easy to *start* dieting. It's hard to *keep* dieting. It's easy to make a decision. It's harder to keep on *taking* the action. So, how do you "Keep on keeping on"? Members of AA know the answer: "One day at a time." If you make it through today, it's more likely you'll make it through tomorrow. You can do it . . . just for today!

~ The difference between ordinary and extraordinary is just a little extra.~

▪ ▪ ▪

CHOICE, HAPPINESS, AND SPAGHETTI SAUCE

Inspiration is everywhere; you just have to *look for it.* Someone once said to me, "Oh, you have to read *Blink*, by Malcolm Gladwell." I got the book, read it, loved it, and looked up Gladwell. He is incredible, and I love his work. I saw that he had done a TED Talk: *Choice, Happiness, and Spaghetti Sauce.* I want choice in my life, I certainly want to be happy, and I'm Italian—always in for some spaghetti sauce—so I watched the TED Talk.

Gladwell is a master storyteller. In the TED Talk, he shared the story of Howard Moskowitz and his study on finding the best spaghetti sauce. Moskowitz was hired by one of the food giants to go and find the best spaghetti sauce out there so that they could make it, perfect it, and be the sales leader in this category. After much research, many tastings, interviews, dinners, and more, Moskowitz did, indeed, find the answer to *Which is the best spaghetti sauce?* Variety! People like variety and choice. We are complex creatures, with many different brains, thoughts, taste buds, sizes, and more. We want to have a choice. He showed similar results for coffee, cars, movies, etc.

So, the magic here is not an acronym this time, but a formula: choice and happiness. When leading others, give people choices and options. Allow for some freedom in their work. In the great Daniel Pink's TED Talk, he shared the big three: Mastery, autonomy, and purpose. These, according to Pink, are the biggest factors in motivating people. The autonomy here is the freedom of choice.

The best leaders allow room for this in their organizations, schools, and teams. I highly recommend watching both TED Talks. If you haven't seen them, they are a must-watch. If you have already watched them, viewing them a second time always adds more to your leadership bucket.

FROM THE SUCCESS HOTLINE ARCHIVES . . .

The one-sentence secret to happiness:

The secret of happiness is to find something more important than you are and dedicate your life to it.

~ Dan Dennett, philosopher

■ ■ ■

AIRTIGHT COMPARTMENTS

D*r. Gilbert called me on a Sunday* and said, "What are you doing Thursday night?"

I said, "I don't have anything—I'll probably be home. What's up?"

"I'm buying you and your wife two tickets to Frank Somma's leadership event in New Jersey." *Wow*, I thought. *This is amazing.* I thanked Doc profusely and shared it with my wife. He's been very generous over the years to me and many others.

Thursday night came, and we were excited. Frank Somma is a good friend of Dr. Gilbert's and is an expert business and leadership coach. Frank was dressed to the nines and ready to lead a great event.

There were so many takeaways from this event about your goals, vision, and getting things done. Frank is a tremendous speaker and sales trainer.

The one that stuck with me the most was *airtight compartments.* How do some people just get stuff done? They seem to have more time than others. *No: they put their time into airtight compartments.* Frank asked that evening for everyone to pretend to be in a submarine. He said, "Imagine that the sub was taking on water, and you were in a room with those doors with the wheel handles in the middle of them; you could shut the doors and spin the wheel to make a vacuum seal. Nothing can get in: no water, no noise, nothing—until you were ready to open them." He said, "Do the same for your work. Seal off the time, and do *only* the one thing you are looking to do."

We live in such a distracted world, with phones, notifications, and constant pulls on our time and attention. Something is always chirping or grabbing at you, especially if you have small children. Even today, while I am writing this excerpt, it is a snow day in my school district, Port Jervis Schools (New York). It is 6:22 a.m., and everyone is sleeping. My phone is away, and all noise and distractions are far from this space. I'll have this beautiful, calm, airtight compartment of time for approximately two more hours. I'll finish this excerpt and most likely one more, and that is all I'll do with this time, besides have some amazing coffee.

Put your deep work, your important work, into airtight compartments. *How, Andrew? I just don't have the time.* Yes, you do; you have to schedule it, and you have to put away the distracting things:

- *Turn off email/social media notifications.*
- *Put the cell phone away/silence. Commit to not looking at it.*
- *Set a timer that you will work in this airtight compartment until then.*
- *Get this time on the schedule, and stick to it.*
- *Get everything you need to work in the airtight compartment: chargers, tools, data, workout equipment. Whatever you need to be in the compartment, get it ready, and have it available.*
- *Schedule the next airtight compartment. It's always good to have something to look forward to.*

I know several people who have written their doctorate on Sunday mornings. Each week, from 6 a.m. until lunchtime, they worked on their doctorate. It took a couple of years, yet they did it. Commit to your airtight compartment, and don't let any water in until you are ready to open those doors. Thank you to Dr. Gilbert for treating me and my wife to attend Frank Somma's leadership event, and thanks to Frank for this excellent leadership tip!

FROM THE SUCCESS HOTLINE ARCHIVES . . .

Frank Somma: Better than Shakespeare, Yogi Berra, and The Bible.

What do I think of when I think of *The Great Frank Somma*?

1. Frank, in the 33 years Success Hotline has been available, you've left me more messages than *any other caller.*
2. You always call on the weekends. You're one of the few who do.
3. You've been quoted on the Hotline more than any other person (that means you beat out Shakespeare, Yogi Berra, and The Bible).

   Here's your famous quote:

   Make a commitment.
   Make it public.
   Make it happen!

4. You also penned another of my all-time favorite quotes . . .

   Your competition's
   name for your #1 customer:
   Their #1 Prospect!

   Frank, you're one of the few who do. You don't just talk the talk—you also walk the talk.

   You're an extraordinary individual.

I don't know how you do all you do—and you do it all with mastery.

I appreciate your brilliance, your assistance, and, most of all, your friendship.

~It is impossible to steal second base
while keeping your foot on first!~

▪ ▪ ▪

FOCUS = FOLLOW ONE COURSE UNTIL SUCCESSFUL

I *have ADHD*. It is a super-turbo brain and spirit that allow me to keep going, keep doing, keep creating. Yet, sometimes it can pull me into the ocean and toss me around for a while, getting me lost in the waves and currents. FOCUS brings me back—the one course, and staying on it. Yes, you have to switch gears sometimes. Yes, you have to add things to what you are doing and where you are going. FOCUS doesn't mean *monotonous*; it means *staying the course*. It means keep grinding, keep going.

In *Outliers*, by Malcolm Gladwell, he shares the 10,000-hour rule: doing something for 10,000 hours to establish mastery. He shares about The Beatles playing in a 24-hour nightclub in Hamburg, Germany, for eight-hour sets at a time, seven days a week. Wow, that is a lot of music. The point is that it was their focus, their one course. What is it that you want to accomplish? How are you going to get there? It worked for The Beatles for sure, honing their craft day after day, until they were ready for their moment to break into stardom. They put in the time, the FOCUS for that opportunity to happen.

I've changed courses several times in my life; as I grew and my positions changed, locations changed, etc. When I was a kid, I wanted to be the best basketball player I could be—I would shoot for days, dribble my ball everywhere I went, sleep with it, and so on. I kept at it. This then shifted to becoming the best husband, teacher, father, basketball official, and more. Things come and go in your life, but when you remain *FOCUSed* on the things you want and the person you want to be, it will open up for you.

I feel so blessed in my life now that I have found that FOCUS, that one thing that I really, really want to do: helping and inspiring people and educators around the world through my speaking, writing, and surviving-and-thriving work. Dr. Gilbert has said this countless times on the Hotline: "If you *really* want to be a champion, then the work is no problem. Well, if you *really* want something, then **FOCUS: F**ollow **o**nly one **c**ourse **u**ntil ***s**uccessful* is not a problem.

Remember, you can try many different things on your course; as long as you keep moving forward, toward that goal, that direction, you'll get there. Keep at it, keep rolling: **FOCUS.**

FROM THE SUCCESS HOTLINE ARCHIVES . . .

Dr. Rob: Golf great Ben Hogan stood over a crucial putt. Suddenly a loud train whistle blared in the distance. After sinking the putt, Hogan was asked if the loud train whistle destroyed his focus.

"*What whistle?*" Hogan replied!

~If you don't stretch your limits, you will set your limits~

■ ■ ■

HOW TO BECOME THE WORLD'S GREATEST STUDENT

by Russell Jones

Russell Jones is a father of four, a granddad of eight. He created *The Top Secrets of Success Interactive Video Series for Kids & Parents* and is the author of two bestselling books—*Top Secrets of Success 4 Kids* and *Sick & Tired of Being Sick & Tired: Solutions for a Better, Healthier Life* as well as *I Did the Best I Could! Ten Critical Anchor Points That Will Equip You & Your Child Now . . . and into the Future.* He is a podcaster, speaker, and master-level health and fitness coach. Russell is also a professional strongman. He does strength feats that very few human beings have ever done!

Russell, in his mid-thirties, lost an infant son and almost lost his wife in a tragic car accident. This forever changed him as a parent and the way he wanted to connect with his children. This is why it has become his life's work to help other parents motivate, encourage, and inspire their children through some of the most challenging years of a young person's life.

▪

This information was shared with me many years ago by one of my favorite elevators, Dr. Rob Gilbert. Of course, an "elevator" is someone who can help you get from where you are to where you want to be faster than you can by yourself.

It was so *simple* that I couldn't believe how powerful it was. It's called "How to Become the World's Greatest Student." Believe it or not, you don't need to be a rocket scientist to be a super-student. But you do need to know the steps. There are only three, and they're simple.

Please note that *simple* is not always *easy*. The good news is that anyone can follow the three steps. But if one refuses to believe, is too lazy, or doesn't want to do anything special with one's life, then, of course, it won't work.

The first step is called *Act as if*. This is all about having the right attitude and being in the right place. *Act as if* you are the world's greatest student.

What does a great student do? Come prepared for class. Sit in the front. Sit up straight. Look awake. Participate in class. Ask questions. Do neat work. Hand in assignments on time. Help others. Have a good attitude.

That's it. That's the first step toward becoming a super-student. Just like positive affirmations, where you speak things about yourself that are going to be true, now you *Act as if* you're already a great student. If you've been a D student all your life, don't expect your grades to change overnight. But plant the *Act as if* seed now, and it will grow into great grades later.

And don't forget that school is really *not* about grades . . . It's about knowledge. Stay hungry to learn new stuff, and you'll stay motivated in school. If you just stay focused *only* on getting good grades, you'll probably get stressed out, and school won't be fun. *Act as if* you've got a great attitude and that you're hungry to learn as much as you can.

One major deterrent to your success in this step is crabs. When you attempt to do something special, the crabs will try to pull you back into the basket.

If you ever visit the ocean and go crabbing, you'll notice that some people act just like crabs. If you catch one crab and put it in a bushel basket, it'll climb right up the side and escape. If you put it back in the basket, it'll climb up the side and escape again. No matter how many times you put it in the basket, it will climb out. But if you put three, four, or five or more crabs into that same basket, as soon as one tries to get out, one will reach up with its claw and grab on tight. Then another crab will grab the second one and hold on for dear life. Then another will grab on, and then another. No crabs can escape. If they would all help each other, they could all escape to freedom. But they won't. They'll die in that basket before they let any one of them get out. Unfortunately, many friends and family can act just like those crabs. I feel sorry for people who act like crabs, but I'm not going to let them keep *me* in *their* basket.

When Dr. Gilbert is talking to young people, he'll remind them that some kids will try to make them believe that being smart in school is not "cool." A lot of kids buy into this lie. They joke about being "dumb" or that they just don't care. The sad part is that, after you leave high school, most people see only about one out of every one hundred kids that they went through school with. Yet so many kids waste years of their lives worrying about what others think of them. Avoid this trap. Get the help you need, forget about what others say, and *Act as if.*

The second step is for you to get a dictionary and have it with you at all times. I know from personal experience that this is a very powerful step. When I was a kid, I developed some really bad habits. One of them was that I didn't read much. When I did read, I didn't really understand some of the words. Because I was lazy, I never took the time to look them up. I mean, if you asked me what a word meant, I could sort of tell you and maybe even use it in a sentence. I just didn't know the *exact* definition, and that's important. So my grades were limited (to C's and D's) because my vocabulary was limited. Because of this, the colleges and universities that I wanted to attend didn't want me. I was fortunate enough to get into a small school and learn the secret. For four years, I carried a dictionary with me. Whenever I could not clearly define a word, out came the dictionary. In the beginning, this was a major pain. Sometimes it would take a long time just to read a sentence. But I knew that I was doing the right thing, and I would pull out that dictionary every time.

The results were phenomenal. In my last three years of college, I received A's in every subject. Both of my parents fainted from the shock. After all the years of being a poor student, I was finally succeeding. I became hungry for knowledge, and good grades just followed. All from a dictionary? Yes, and the patience to greatly improve my life. *Have one with you at all times.* Don't leave home without it.

The third step is just as simple as the others. Commit two to three hours every day to improving yourself. Time actually in school doesn't count. You can include homework time. Just tell yourself, "Look, most kids are going to school, doing as little work as possible, and then goofing off whenever they can. If I want to really be special, I'll need to do something different. If all it takes is a few hours a day, I'll go for it."

What if I get done with my homework at school, or if I don't get any homework at all? What if there's no school? What about on weekends or summer vacations? The deal is *every day*, 365 days per year. This is not punishment, and it'll be a lot of fun. Have a bunch of great books lined up, or get started on special projects for school or in your community.

I know that this stuff works because it worked for me. If I could change from being a lazy, unmotivated, loser student to one of the "world's greatest students," so can you. Now that you have a plan for success, all you have to do is choose to start and then be "too tough to quit." The fun you'll have doing great things with your life will be tremendously rewarding.

Exit Note: We all have different ways to learn things quickly. Many times, the way we are taught in school does not fit our personal learning style very well. It's frustrating to see some get straight A's in school with hardly any effort. It can make you feel dumb and not too smart. But that's a lie . . . unless you believe it.

I know many brilliant people who really struggled in school yet went on to have amazingly successful lives. Just don't give up trying to find your way. School is important for your foundation, but as you've been learning here, there is a ton more to learn outside of school as well. If I can conquer the school thing, you can, too.

Thanks, Dr. Gilbert! The parents, family, and friends of Russell Jones appreciate you to the highest levels!

FROM THE SUCCESS HOTLINE ARCHIVES . . .

Dr. Gilbert's 10 Rules for College Success

#1. Show up.

#2: Pay attention.

#3. Ask questions.

#4. Ask for help.

#5. Help others.

#6. Take great notes.

#7. Do the work whether you feel like it or not!

#8. Do not cheat.

#9. *Do Not Quit!*

#10. Call the Success Hotline every day!!!

~It is not how great the opportunity is.
It is how great you are to the opportunity.~
~Fazio, Success Hotline caller~

■ ■ ■

THE 7 C'S

D*r.* ***Gilbert loves streaks and challenges.*** Over the years, he has had many: The New Year's challenge, the Dr. Terrie update streak, the Presidential memorization challenge, the free-throw challenge, etc. The 7 C's have probably been the biggest, most consistent challenge. Each summer, Dr. Rob has motivated us to eat better and be better by *not* eating these junk food items, and he cleverly named it the 7-C Challenge.

From Memorial Day to Labor Day, Doc challenged the callers to *not* eat: Chips, Cola, Chocolate, Candy, Cake, Cookies. *Whaaaaaaat?* Really? Are you kidding? *I was liking this book until I read that.* Is that what you're thinking? Was that your reaction?

Wait. That is only six C's . . . Chips, Cola, Chocolate, Candy, Cake, Cookies. The seventh is *Complaining.* Give it up. I gave up these 7 C's multiple years in a row. It made me realize the high amount of sugar I was eating. It felt great to cut that out. It's good to put some limits on yourself. You will look better, feel better physically, and feel proud knowing you had the discipline to give up all that junk.

Honestly, since I gave up the 7 C's, I haven't wanted to eat those things anymore. Good thing the list is C's and not P's. If it were ***pizza*** we're talking about, we'd have a problem!

Dr. Gilbert has always modeled growth over the years, too. After sharing the 7 C's for many years, he added to it. Now, it's called the 8 C's. Yes, he added an 8th: Complimenting. He realized, after a Hotline caller pointed it out, that it needed to be more positive. The

7 C's are about withholding; the 8th C provides a way for you to be proactive, to take action. Complimenting someone can energize you while making someone else feel better, so it officially became the "8 C's Challenge"! I love it! Thanks, Dr. Rob, for dialing me in each and every year!

#TrueStory: I met Dr. Rob in New Jersey for coffee one afternoon before a speaking engagement. We sat down at a local New Jersey diner, and while Dr. Rob was setting the books down he'd brought for me, I ordered a coffee. He then ordered a Coke. *This was* not *during the 7 C's season.* I said loudly, "A Coke!?! What? Dr. Rob drinks soda? *Really?*" I said to him. I was shocked. He quickly changed his drink to tea.

We chatted about it for a bit and then moved on. About six months later, while on the phone, he shared that he hadn't had a Coke since that day. What day? I had forgotten about the interaction, *but he hadn't.*

Dr. Rob shared that he felt like he had let me down as a friend and Hotline caller, and he knew he shouldn't have Coke, so he cut it. He stopped immediately and never went back.

Now, *that* is commitment, *that* is action, *that* is living what he says each and every day on the Hotline. It also made me realize that my words and my actions *matter.* Just like Dr. Rob made me *believe and feel* that I could write a book, I did the same for him—making him feel like, "I shouldn't have this cola," in a good, action-producing way.

It's true: People will forget what you said and forget what you did, but they will never forget how you made them *feel*—good *and* bad! Good luck with the 8 C's, friends. It's a great tradition, and I highly recommend you do it! Like Dr. Rob has asked many times over the years: "At the end of the 8 C's Challenge on Labor Day, will you say—'I'm *glad* I did'? or 'I *wish* I had'?"

FROM THE SUCCESS HOTLINE ARCHIVES . . .

"It's not how much time you put into it; it's what you put *into* the time!"

~*"Your thoughts determine what you want. Your actions determine what you'll get."*~

~Fazio, Success Hotline caller

■ ■ ■

CHAPTER 6

ACTION

Do it!

Do it right!!

Do it right now!!!

~Dr. Rob Gilbert

The Magic

ACRONYMS, FORMULAS, & IMPACTFUL STORIES

of Leadership

A Tribute to the Amazing Dr. Rob Gilbert *& the Success Hotline*

WIN

D*r. Gilbert often talks about* being a winner, winning, etc., on the Hotline. Yet, this WIN is an acronym. How are you growing? How are you learning? What are you doing for yourself each and every day? Even right now, as I write this, I've created a WIN in my day—WIN: **w**hat **I n**eed. When you take/make WIN time in your life, you'll accomplish more of what you want to accomplish. WIN time is for you, and you can design it however you want.

So, how do you create WIN time? Easy—schedule it. Sit down in a quiet space, and schedule it. With this book project (Thanks, Dr. Gilbert, for the *Magic Acronyms* book!!!), I write from 6:30 a.m. to 7:15 a.m. daily. I really wanted to write this book and was excited about it, yet I was being pulled in other directions—setting up my podcast, prepping for my speaking engagements, following up on emails, etc. The *book* is what I wanted, and here I am writing during WIN time. The acronym WIN feels good and sounds good, and I enjoy my WIN time.

Exercise is also a WIN-win—*what I need.* How many times have we said it? "I should exercise more. I am going to exercise more. I am going to get back to exercising." I've been there, wrestled with these thoughts, and struggled to put on those shoes. Now, I've got it. It is WIN time—**w**hat **I n**eed. Just like we sit down for dinner or put gas in the car (or plug in the electric!). These are things you do regularly because you *need* them. Well, so is exercise. So what is that special project or that thing you want to do that's been calling you? For me, it is this book and tribute to Dr. Gilbert. I collect wins every day during WIN time because I schedule it, plan it, and, when WIN time comes during my day, I execute it. I even use this timer to keep me on schedule and focused on my schedule.

That is how I treat my WIN time, like Frank Somma shared in Chapter 5—Airtight Compartments. Nothing in or out, just the work I am doing at that time. It is *my* time, and I get to decide what that WIN time looks like, feels like, and what it accomplishes, because it is: ***What-I-Need!***

FROM THE SUCCESS HOTLINE ARCHIVES . . .

Not enough time?

Dr. Rob: Medical school is not easy. You go to school all day, and you study all night. Roger Bannister wanted to be a doctor. But he also wanted to be the first person to ever run a mile in under four minutes. Every day, he cut a different one of his medical-school classes and went to the track, where he met his coach. How much do you have to train to do something that no one has ever done before? Roger trained only 40–45 minutes a day. That's it!

And on May 6, 1954, Roger Bannister ran a mile in 3 minutes 59.4 seconds.

It's not how much
time you put in—
it's what you put
into the time.

~Just do it.~
~NIKE~

■ ■ ■

MY OLD BLUE CHAIR

L*ook up the lyrics* to Kenny Chesney's "Old Blue Chair." (I would have included them, but I am not sure if I can reprint them without permission.) I thoroughly enjoy Kenny Chesney's music, the message, and the whole vibe of "No Shoes Nation." One song in particular that gets my attention is titled "Old Blue Chair." Put the book down for a moment, grab your phone, and read the lyrics. The "Old Blue Chair" is Kenny's place to write, reflect, think, grow, and more. He compares the "Old Blue Chair" to a trusted friend and writes, *"I've read a lot of books, and I wrote a few songs. Looked at my life—where it is going, where it's gone."* It is his spot where the magic happens.

Where is your "Old Blue Chair"? Where can you go to get away from it all? Hit pause, be quiet, and get that deep thinking we need. Calling the Hotline each day is certainly magic, but it is only three minutes. To really process and put into action the things Dr. Gilbert has stressed on the Hotline, you have to create some deep-thinking time, some quiet planning time. You can't just run around doing all these magic formulas and acronyms.

My family is a busy family—two parents working, three kids heavily involved in school and sports, an active dog, a wood-burning fireplace, and more. I am very comfortable at home, but I'm focused on the things for my home and my family. It is a challenge to "do" the items written in this book when I am home. Indeed, at 5 a.m., I can get to many of these things, but it is at the "Old Blue Chair" in my life that I can get to my goals and work.

I have three of them. It took a while to figure them out, and I had to try several different places, times, etc. The first spot was a small Airbnb close to my home and work. Yes, it's close. Most of the time, when we go to an Airbnb, we go "away." No, this was close.

The magic formula for me was to leave after work on a Friday and get to the Airbnb. I'd write from late afternoon to eight or nine p.m. Get to bed early and up at 5 a.m. Working out, great coffee, and right back to writing again. I'd write straight until about 11-ish a.m. and take a short break. I'd go for a walk, stretch, and write some more. My wife would join me at around 3 p.m. or so. We would walk together and grab a bite to eat, and then she would have her quiet time, her "Old Blue Chair," and I'd head home to be with the kids and family. She would spend the night and be home for family dinner on Sunday. This worked for us for a few years until this amazing Airbnb stopped renting.

I found two more places—the second was a Marriott. When I travel and speak, I always stay at a Marriott. Actually, as I write this, I am in Illinois, heading to a school to present. I arrived a few hours earlier, got an early check-in, and got a takeout dinner. I have been writing for the past few hours. It's quiet; it has good WiFi, good lighting, and a comfortable chair (pun intended). I am now taking the time as I can get it, adding it to my trips. The third is on an airplane. It's great. I work "off-line" on the plane because the Wi-Fi is so spotty, but I set up a number of documents or presentations I can work on, get into my seat, and literally buckle up, allowing me to work uninterrupted. Headphones and horse blinders (well, not really, but yes to the headphones)—I am locked in, literally, with nowhere to go.

These three spaces work for me—but what works for you?

Andrew—I don't travel as much as you, and I want to work on that special project and my goals.

Do It!

How about the local coffee shop? Do they open early on Saturday or Sunday? Get there at 5:30 or 6:00 a.m., and carve out that time. Can you go to your office on the weekend? I know many a school administrator who got their doctorates by working on it Saturday and Sunday mornings from 5 to 8 a.m. over the course of a couple of years! Even the local library. Grab one of those old-fashioned study-carrels. You can get in there and get to it—uninterrupted—your goals, your dreams, your magic acronyms, formulas, and stories.

Find your "Old Blue Chair" in your life, and make it happen.

FROM THE SUCCESS HOTLINE ARCHIVES . . .

Dr. Rob: The country music songs mentioned most often on Success Hotline:

1. "The Gambler" by Kenny Rogers
2. "I Love" by Tom T. Hall
3. "Come from the Heart" by Kathy Mattea
4. "Unanswered Prayers" by Garth Brooks
5. "The Blind Man in the Bleachers" by Kenny Starr
6. "Friends in Low Places" by Garth Brooks
7. "I Will Always Love You" by Dolly Parton
8. "A Boy Named Sue" by Johnny Cash
9. "The Greatest" by Kenny Rogers
10. "Chattahoochee" by Alan Jackson

"Sometimes you don't realize how true country songs are until you find yourself in the middle of one."

~Hank Williams, Jr.

~*"There's a blue rocking chair/Sitting in the sand/Weathered by the storms/And well-oiled hands."*~

~Kenny Chesney~

■ ■ ■

THE THREE FROGS

by Mark Housel

Mark Housel is the owner of Housel Fun & Fitness. He is the retired 2020 New Jersey Physical Education Teacher of the Year and the author of *What Kind of Teacher Do You Want to Be?* Mark is an energizing, motivational, fit, and fun educator who has influenced countless students—and now teachers—by inspiring them with his positive and contagious energy.

▪

In 2018, I was at the NJAHPERD Lake Conference in Johnsonburg, New Jersey. One of the presenters mentioned the Success Hotline. He described it very well when he said, "If you want to get better at anything in life, then call the Success Hotline." That day, I called, and I have been calling ever since. Dr. Gilbert and the Success Hotline have changed my life.

I wasn't happy with where I was headed back in 2018. There was too big a gap between who I was and who I wanted to be in many aspects of my life. Since I started calling the Success Hotline in 2018, I have been named the 2020 New Jersey Elementary Physical Education Teacher of the Year and the 2023 SHAPE America Eastern District Teacher of the Year. That made me one of five finalists for the National PE Teacher of the Year. In 2021, I was hired as an adjunct professor at Monmouth University to teach future Health and PE teachers. I have become a national teacher-workshop presenter, and, over the past couple of years, I have visited thirteen states to present workshops on teaching. Since calling the Hotline, I have published two children's books, and in May 2024, I published the book *What Kind of Teacher Do You Want to Be?*

My life wasn't changed right away when I called the Hotline. If there is any fine print to the Success Hotline, it's this: change won't happen without your consent, and it won't happen without you *taking action*. Dr. Gilbert doesn't show up in your life and do the work for you. There is no magic wand that he waves. What he does is constantly and consistently challenge you to take action. Because of Dr. Gilbert, I actually cannot speak to someone for more than 10 minutes without reciting an inspirational quote of his or telling one of his stories. Trying to nail down which Dr. Gilbert quote, story, or point that has meant the most to me would be nearly impossible. So, I picked the point that I use the most when I am trying to impact others.

Since I started calling the Hotline, my proudest accomplishment by far is working with my Monmouth University students. Each time we have class, I ask them the same question that inspired me to write my book *What Kind of Teacher Do You Want to Be?* In fact, I ask this same question of teachers all around the country when I present workshops. Insert any word in the place of "teachers." What kind of plumber do you want to be, what kind of son, friend, mother, accountant? No one—*no one*—is *ever* going to answer this question with, "average," or "below average," or "ehhhhh!" Yet we all have seen or know these kinds of teachers and people, haven't we?

I always follow up this question with Dr. Gilbert's Three Frogs Riddle:

Three frogs sat on a log. One decided to jump off; how many are left?

(Please think about this before reading on below.)

The answer is three. Why? Because *deciding to jump off* the log and *jumping off* the log are two completely different things. So are *deciding* to be the kind of person you want to be and *becoming* that person.

Into Action:

- Deciding to change is an important step for making changes in your life.
- We can decide all we want, all day long. We can make a hundred decisions about what we want in life. However, until we act on those decisions, we are going to be left on the log with those other three frogs.

I want to leave you with a quick story of what happened to me at the amazing IAHPERD convention near Chicago, Illinois, in December 2024. I was presenting a workshop for a couple hundred teachers, and I asked if anyone had heard of the Success Hotline. Someone in the crowd yelled out, "Success Leaves Clues!" I stopped everything and immediately went over to speak with him. This teacher has been calling the Success Hotline for years because he met Brian Cain, another one of the contributing authors in this book, at a baseball conference. If you want to be successful, you will get clues from the success master, Dr. Gilbert, every single day.

My book has a whole chapter devoted to Dr. Gilbert and the Success Hotline. If you want to find out more about it, please go to https://houselfitness.com/wkot1 or scan the code:

FROM THE SUCCESS HOTLINE ARCHIVES . . .

Dr. Rob: *Procrastinating???*

Read this:

How do you get started? By getting started!

Don't wait until you *feel* like getting started. You get started by getting started.

You get started by taking *action.*

How did you get out of bed this morning? Most people physically force themselves to get out of bed even when they don't feel like it.

If you waited until you felt like it—you'd probably still be in bed!

You start by taking that first step, even if it's a baby step. Put your body in motion, and the emotions will follow.

Don't wait until you feel like doing it. Do it—then it's more likely you'll feel like it.

Take that first step.

Now!

~Good times pass. Bad times pass. The commitment remains.~

■ ■ ■

ABRACADABRA

I ***heard Doc say this a few times***, and then I heard it again from Dr. Gilbert's protégé Mark Glicini: The actual translation of "Abracadabra" means, *"I create as I speak."* What—when I speak, I *create*? Really? Because I can say anything I want? So it's not magic?

I just have to think about it and make it happen. *Yes!* Yes, this is true. This is so true. For years, I've heard "Abracadabra," and I thought it was magic, like make-believe. If you adopt this mindset of "I create as I speak," you will work to make it happen. And no, it is not the snap of a finger or a wave of a wand, but it is a crazy focus, an intentional list, a desired outcome, and you fiercely working at this goal! Yes, it can be, if you really want it. If it is to be, it is up to me—#true. With my words (goals, focus, vision, you fill in the blank), *I will create*. This is so very true.

As I turn the page to fifty years old in my life, I wish I had understood this concept at twenty. At twenty, I used to tell myself "That can't be me." Now, at fifty, I ask myself, why *not* me? Abracadabra—*I create as I speak*. Keep creating, friends. It is *not* magic—**it is you!**

FROM THE SUCCESS HOTLINE ARCHIVES . . .

Dr. Rob: Once upon a time, there was a young man who dreamed of becoming a knight for King Arthur's Knights of the Round Table. Before he could become a knight, he had to pass one last test—he had to slay a dragon. The young man was scared to death. He asked one of the knights what he should do about his tremendous fear.

This knight advised him to see Merlin the Magician, because Merlin had a magic sword.

When the young man told Merlin about his problem, Merlin vanished and then reappeared with a beautiful, gilded sword. Merlin then instructed him, "This sword is magic, and the day that you go out to slay your dragon, come see me, and I will give you this magic sword. But make sure that your scabbard is empty. And remember: This sword will work its magic only if you are in danger."

One week later, the would-be knight returned. He was dressed for battle, and, as Merlin had instructed, his scabbard was empty. Merlin told the young man to close his eyes, and Merlin put the magic sword into his scabbard.

As the young man left, Merlin reminded him, "Remember, this sword will work its magic only if you are in danger." The young man, now more confident than ever, rode his horse out onto the plains, where he confronted his dragon. It was a fierce battle. The dragon was breathing fire. The dragon's tail knocked the young man off his trusty steed. The young man was on the ground, and the dragon came in for the kill.

Just at that moment, the young man remembered the magic sword. He took the sword out of his scabbard and started slashing the dragon's legs. The dragon was hurt and fell down. The young man jumped onto the dragon and put the sword into the dragon's heart, killing the dragon.

The young man returned home victorious. The first person he went to see was Merlin. He told Merlin about how the magic sword saved his life. As he took it out of his scabbard to return it, he looked at it in amazement and said, "Merlin, this isn't the magic sword. This isn't the same sword you showed me last week. This isn't that beautiful, gilded magic sword. It's just an ordinary sword!"

Merlin nodded and said, "There is no magic sword. ***The magic is believing!***"

~The person who says it can't be done will be passed by the person doing it.~

■ ■ ■

DSB

D*o* ***simple better.*** Not much to write or explain here. This one is easy. Do the little things often, and do them well. Do simple better. Life is short. When you are consistently doing little things after little things well, they add up. It's like saving money and stacking wins. After a while, you have a lot. What kind of things are we talking about? Here are a few examples:

- *Show up. Not just on time—but early.* ***Do simple better.***
- *Do more than expected. This is a Gilbert favorite. When the boss asks you to do x, you do X +2. When you do more, you expect more of yourself. When you expect more of yourself, you do more.* ***Do simple better.***
- *Smile, and say "Please" and "Thank you."* ***Do simple better.***
- *Ask people about themselves. We tend to talk about ourselves too often. Ask others about themselves, their passions, and what they are working on. Be an active listener, and let them talk. It is a simple interaction, yet you will do it better.* ***Do simple better.***
- *Get back to others: emails, RSVPs, things you said you would do. Confirm, follow up, remind, and more. It's simple.* ***Do simple better.***
- *Be empathetic. Let others know that you feel for them and care for them. Give them a hug, a card, or an impromptu visit.* ***Do simple better.***

- *Be prepared. Get your stuff in order. Carve out the time you need to be ready. Check your equipment, your mind, your body, your presentation, your project, your spirit. Be prepared. Be ready.* ***Do simple better.***

The list could go on and on. There are so many simple things that we can do—just do them just a little bit better. That little bit better can take you a long way.

FROM THE SUCCESS HOTLINE ARCHIVES . . .

Inch by inch,
It's a cinch.
Yard by yard,
It might be hard.

~Life is a marathon, not a sprint. Keep moving forward.~

■ ■ ■

THE SUCCESS CYCLE

I *love all of Dr. Gilbert's messages.* This is one of my favorites, the success cycle:

- *The more you do something, the better you get.*
- *The better you get, the better you feel, and the more you like it.*
- *The more you like it, the more you do it.*

The more you do it, the better you get, the more you like . . . and so on. The cycle continues. *The success cycle.* How true is this? Think about something you're really good at. You probably weren't that good at this when you started. How did you improve? You improved by doing it over and over.

For me, whether it's public speaking, being a principal, or officiating college basketball—all of these loves of mine went through the success cycle. I wasn't very good at *any* of them when I started, but slowly, and I mean *slowly,* I grew and improved through the success cycle. Then, when I heard Dr. Gilbert talk about it on the Hotline, it put the cycle on speed mode. It motivated me even more to get better at what I was doing.

I am proud that this sign hangs in our high school in Port Jervis, NY! Let's put it into action here for you in this book. What is that thing that you want to improve, grow in? Write it down right now. Put these steps into action today!

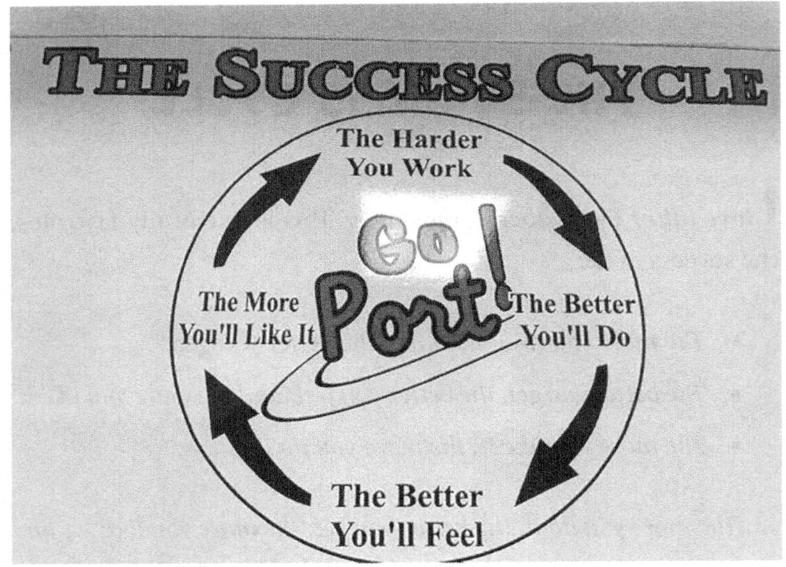

1. How can you *do* this activity more? The more you do it, the better you will get, so create three ways to do it *more.* Put it/them on your calendar, and schedule it (very important.)
2. How did you improve? Each time out—each podcast you do, each song you write, or each lesson you teach, find a few things that feel new and improved to you. Write them down, and do them again next time.
3. Rate yourself each time out. Make a simple scale from one to ten. How did you do? You can get really specific and make a rubric, or you can just grade yourself by feel: How did it look and sound? Now, maybe ask someone else to grade you—and get specific feedback from a trusted person.
4. Add a new tool, line, or strategy: smile more, pause in between, etc. If it is writing, maybe add a standing desk. Mix it up. Will

one of these changes help you improve? If it is working out early in the morning, try adding brighter lights or a heater. Watch a YouTube video to learn and try a new technique.

All of these minor tweaks can add to your experience and make it better. Ultimately, it is just consistently doing that *thing* repeatedly that makes you improve. 100%. The success cycle is a proven strategy that consistently will yield the results you want in your life.

FROM THE SUCCESS HOTLINE ARCHIVES . . .

The Three-Word Success Course

Everything you need to know about success can be reduced to three simple words:

CAN. WILL. NOW.

1. **Can**. *Can you?* Can you actually do it? Do you possess the innate ability? The truth: Yes, you can! You have the same inborn ability as an Edison or an Einstein. They weren't born with any more raw talent than you were. You have superpowers inside you. Just because you haven't discovered them yet doesn't mean they are not there. They are there! They do exist!
2. **Will**. *Will you* actualize this remarkable ability of yours? Just because you *can* do something does not necessarily mean that you *will*. You have the same raw ability as Shakespeare. But what did Shakespeare do that you might not have done yet? Through remarkable effort, perseverance, and commitment,

Shakespeare gained access to his remarkable ability. You can, too!

3. **Now**. *When will you start?* Many people die with their songs inside them—unwritten and unsung. Right *now*, take one step (even if it's a tiny baby step) in the direction of your dreams. Action inspires!

~Don't curse the darkness. Light a candle!~

▪ ▪ ▪

OADB

D*r. Gilbert has said this one a lot*—and it is so, so true. **O**n **a** **d**aily **b**asis. What is that thing that you want to do? Whatever it is, do it *on a daily basis.* The habits we live each and every day help shape our lives. Pause reading right now, and grab a pen. Make two lists: What are the things that you do *every day* that help shape who you are—good or bad? Now, write down the habits you wish you did each day to be more consistent.

Doing those habits each and every day helps you stack—stacking money, stacking exercise, stacking eating healthfully, stacking reading fifteen minutes each night, etc., etc., etc. Writing this book has been a great time challenge for me. I had to fight for time with all that I had going on in my life during this time (three busy teenagers in the house, along with my full-time job, speaking, blogging, podcasting, and more). I committed to writing at least one excerpt per day to get the project completed.

Halfway through 2024, I got away from writing. I was really busy with speaking and some other inspirational projects. I felt like I was getting pulled further and further away from writing this book, until one day, I said, *"Enough."* I would write 30 minutes each morning and finish one excerpt daily. Period. No excuses; no other work during that time. *Bam! OADB!* And then it happened. I got on a roll, finishing the book in 2025, and here it is, in your hands now. Why? How? *OADB*—that's how.

And what do we do *when we don't feel like it?* We do it anyway. People can look at others who have achieved a lot and say, "Wow, they got it easy" or "It came easy to them." No. Fake news. They achieved a lot because they continued the course even when they didn't feel like it. Dr. Gilbert has often said, "If it is easy to do, it is also easy *not* to do." #Soverytrue. The habit that you do each day to grow, learn, and get stronger might not always be easy, but make sure you do it. *OADB*. **O**n **a** **d**aily **b**asis. Keep stacking those wins. Keep stacking those positive habits. Keep writing, keep being alcohol-free, keep that bedtime, keep that workout time, and more. When it is all said and done, will you be glad you did or wish you had? *OADB*.

FROM THE SUCCESS HOTLINE ARCHIVES . . .

Elephant Eating

Dr. Rob: Whether you want to get all A's in school, make more money in sales, or become a star athlete . . . you have to know *how to eat an elephant. An elephant*???

Question:

How do you eat an elephant?

Answer:

One bite at a time.

In the words of Little Big Man, a Success Hotline caller,

"It's better to do *a little a lot* than to do *a lot a little.*"

It's more effective to practice or study two hours a day for five straight days than to study ten hours for one day.

But you've got to do it *every day—every single day.*

So, eat your elephant one bite at a time, but make sure you take a bite every single day!

~If I miss three days of practice, my audience will know it.
If I miss two days, my critics will know it.
If I miss one day, I know it.~

~Ignace Paderewski, pianist~

■ ■ ■

HATS

I*n 2022, I wrote HATS* with Jay Billy and Brian McCann, two incredible school leaders, Jay from New Jersey and Brian from Massachusetts. It stands for *Heartfelt Acts for Teachers, Students, and Staff.* Now, maybe you're reading this and saying, "I'm not a teacher or educator, so how can this benefit me?" It can. Stick with me.

The concept of HATS came from my friend Jay. Each day, Jay would wear a different hat at the arrival and departure of the school buses. Literally, he has hundreds of hats in his office and picks a different one for each occasion, morning and afternoon. I heard this and loved it. *Wow*—how kind, how authentic. It truly is a heartfelt act. Then, the acronym "downloaded" in my head. Jon Gordon, the great leader and author, coined that phrase. *Capture the downloads.* I did just that. HATS: Heartfelt Acts for Teachers, Students, and Staff was born and bloomed into a book.

So, how does this help you if you're not an educator? HATS is for everyone. Regardless of your work, passions, and more, giving or doing HATS for others is what it is all about. Dr. Gilbert has shared this over and over—*it is about others.* The whole Success Hotline is one big HAT that he does each and every day. Doing kind and impactful things for others and helping them along the way only fills your bucket.

Here are a couple of examples I share in the book:

Emailing people only during their contractual hours: A simple-yet-meaningful act that can positively impact people. And one of the best parts is they don't even know you are doing it. They might get the email on Monday at 8:30 a.m., yet you wrote on Sunday at 2 p.m. It's not a big deal, but if you had sent it right when you wrote it, maybe that person would have stopped spending time with their family or, even worse, started overthinking your request or the content of the email. In essence, you could be stealing time from them when it could have just waited until a workday.

The power of the handwritten note: An email, a text, a quick thank-you at the water cooler. We all do it, but I challenge you to think about the power of the handwritten note. It is old-school, yet still the most powerful, thoughtful gesture. Dr. Gilbert has highly recommended handwritten notes many times on the Success Hotline. It is authentic and leaves a lasting impact. Get some nice note paper, some cards, and send the notes. Yes, now it is too expensive to mail, and it takes too long to get there, but do it. Write the notes. They matter and will impact that other person.

FROM THE SUCCESS HOTLINE ARCHIVES . . .

The Difference That Makes the Difference

Dr. Rob: On Thanksgiving, just about everyone in the small town went to the traditional high school football game.

At half-time of the big game, the football team from 1982 was honored. They were the only team in the school's history to win a state championship. That Saturday night, the class of '82 had their 25th reunion. It was there that former teammates Jack and Leo finally got a chance to talk about the good old days. They hadn't seen each other since graduation. Jack, the All-State quarterback, had gone on to become one of the most successful and powerful CEOs in the country.

After Leo graduated from college, he returned home and became the minister at a local church.

"Leo, I want to thank you for making me the success I am today," the businessman said.

"Jack, stop pulling my leg!" the minister said with a laugh. "From what I've read, you run a huge corporation. I didn't have anything to do with that, and we haven't seen each other in years."

"You never knew this, Leo, but when we were in high school, I was incredibly jealous of you."

"Me? Jack, *you* were the golden boy. All the big-time colleges were recruiting you. All the girls wanted to go out with you. And your name was in the paper every day."

"That may have been true, Leo, but here's what you didn't know. Even with all my honors and awards, you had the one thing I always wanted the most. The guys on the team elected you captain. I may have been the star of the team, but you were the captain of the team."

"I never knew that you cared about that," Leo said.

"I certainly did! It bothered me so much that, just before graduation, I asked Coach why the guys on the team voted for you—and not me. Coach told me something I've never forgotten. He said, 'Jack, you're the best player I've ever coached. Leo doesn't have the kind of talent you have. But here's the difference. Jack, you were the best player **on the team**, but Leo was the best player **for the team**. You wanted to be the **best player** in the state, while Leo wanted to make us the **best team** in the state.'"

"You know, Leo, it was tough hearing that from Coach," the CEO admitted. "He was being so blunt, and I knew he was telling me the truth. I was **selfish**, and you were always **selfless**—and everyone knew it. Everyone could see it every day at practice. That's why everyone voted for you. It's a lesson I had to learn and it's a lesson I've never forgotten. You see, Coach was right. The difference between us is that, for me, it was all about '*me*,' and for you, it was all about '*we*.'

"After we graduated, I worked hard to become more like you. As a matter of fact, thanks to you, I was voted captain of my college team my junior and senior years. And what Coach told me also helped me to quickly climb the corporate ladder. "The 'old me' would have wanted my company to be the best company **in** the world," Jack said. "Now I strive to make my company the best company **for** the world. Leo, that's why I need to thank you."

"I want to thank you, too, Jack" the minister said warmly.

"For what?"

"You just wrote tomorrow's sermon for me!"

~It's more important to be the
best person for the team
than to be the
best person on the team.~

■ ■ ■

BTDT

M*y oldest daughter is a teenager.* I love watching her grow into the young lady she's becoming. As many of you who have teenagers know, watching their choices of self-expression is also very beautiful. It can be challenging at times, but watching their creative spirits blossom on the journey of "teenage-hood" is certainly interesting.

One day in her room, I saw a poster of the musical artist Pitbull. I'm a fan of Pitbull. I like his energy and his music. I also enjoy the stories I've heard of his work ethic and how he runs his business. I've heard him refer to himself as "Mr. Worldwide" multiple times in both his speech and in his music.

As I looked at the quote on the wall and said the words out loud, "Been there. Done that," this thought is where my mind went to immediately: *If you've been there and done that, then you have to go there and do this.* There's so much out there to do and accomplish, and sometimes our fears hold us back. If Pitbull has been there and done that, he surely has gone there and done it. Also, it can be hard going through these things for the first time.

In my book *Tales from the Hardwood*, I share a lot of personal firsts. I talk about when I officiated college basketball for the first time at the Division I level. My first time at Madison Square Garden, my first time at Duke University, my first time ejecting a coach, and my first NCAA NIT game. All of these were such grand experiences for me, and I was so proud looking back at all of them that I had *been there and done that.* In those moments, going through them for the first time was challenging, and I was certainly nervous. All of that is normal, and no one said it would be easy.

As you read this book and on your own leadership journey, I challenge you to *go there and do that*, whatever *there* is and what *that* may be in your life. When you look back, it's the things that we didn't do most of the time that bring us regret. Go out there and do it!

But Andrew, I've never done that before, and I'm not sure how. There is a first for everything, and like Dr. Gilbert says in Chapter 8, it is the start that stops most people.

Next time you find yourself jamming to some Pitbull, think about the concept that *he's been there and done that.* That's a whole lot of doing *and* a whole lot of experience. Get going.

FROM THE SUCCESS HOTLINE ARCHIVES . . .

Shock the World

Dr. Rob: Many years ago, the University of Michigan's men's basketball team met heavyweight champion Muhammad Ali in an airport. After all his super-excited players got Ali's autograph and had pictures taken with him, the coach said, "Champ, what advice do you have for my team?"

Ali said only three words, "Shock the world!" Ali knew that you don't become the heavyweight champion of the world or the NCAA basketball champion team by holding back.

Here's the story of a young woman who shocked the world!

At a small high school in Tennessee, there was a special graduation ceremony ritual. After being handed a diploma, each graduate went to the microphone and told the audience about his or her future plans. One boy said he was going to work on his dad's farm. Applause. One girl said she was going to attend the local community college. Applause. Another girl said she was going to Nashville to become a country music star. Applause from her parents and relatives, but most of the others in the audience snickered and laughed.

Many years later, the same girl said that, whenever she felt like quitting, she remembered the taunting laughter at graduation and said, "I'll show them." They're all applauding her now—because her name is Dolly Parton.

The basic difference between
an ordinary person
and a warrior is that
a warrior takes everything as a challenge,
while an ordinary person takes everything
as a blessing or a curse."

~ Carlos Castaneda, author

~To be a champion, you have to believe in yourself
when no one else does.~

~Sugar Ray Robinson, boxer~

■ ■ ■

DMTE

If there were a Top Ten of Success Hotline sayings, this one would definitely be in it. This could be in the top five, maybe even the top three: *Do More Than Expected.* So simple, yet so vast. There are opportunities everywhere to do more than expected. Think about where you are right now to do more than expected. What could it be?

Maybe you are at the pool in the summer, reading this book. You could, in the next few minutes:

- *Compliment the staff of the place you are at.*
- *Pick up a piece of trash on your way to the restroom.*
- *Buy someone you don't know a cold refreshment.*
- *Smile at someone while walking by.*

How about at work? Tons of examples.

- *Bagels for people you work with on Fridays.*
- *A public compliment/acknowledgment of the custodial or maintenance staff.*
- *Cancel the next staff meeting, and tell people they could take the time to get fresh air, take a walk, etc.*

Doing more than expected is many times free, pleasing to others, and makes you feel good. Dr. Gilbert shares this concept in addition to helping others, but also helping yourself, improving your work ethic. He shares about the great Melissa Sapio, his top student of all time. You'll find out more about her below.

When you consistently do more than expected, you are building up that muscle—the muscle of *doing more*. I share the example of taking a picture of or with a student in school. If you're an educator, how many times have you done this? Countless. Average: post it on the website or social media to recognize the student. Very nice, yet that is the norm. Do more than expected: Post the picture on the website and social media, and then:

- *Stop at your local Walmart or pharmacy and print out the picture. It will cost you about 40 cents.*
- *Sign the picture and put the date on it, saying, "Great job at the _____ event. So proud of you."*
- *Mail it to the child and the parents with a short note saying how proud you are of that student and how you can really see them going places. Offer some other words of specific encouragement.*
- *Send the picture with a short note to the local paper or media outlet, celebrating the student sharing some positive words about her or him.*
- *Hang the picture on a bulletin board at school, acknowledging their achievement.*

In the digital world we live in, glossy photos on paper are becoming a lost art. Do you see how these simple acts above can have such a profound and positive compounding effect on a young person's life? Maybe the student hangs the picture in their room and sees it daily as inspiration and then goes on to college to study chemical biology and find the cure for cancer, all because you *did more than expected* and motivated that child. It *can* happen and *does* happen all the time. *Do more than expected* to help yourself and others.

FROM THE SUCCESS HOTLINE ARCHIVES . . .

Dr. Rob: I've taught at Montclair State University for more than 45 years. During that time, I had more than 12,000 students in my courses. Of all those students, only one graduated with a perfect 4.0 average. Her name was Melissa Sapio, now Dr. Melissa Sapio. She took 44 courses and got 44 A's. She never received even one A-. Melissa still comes back to Montclair to give guest lectures to my students. Here's what she says, "I'm no smarter than you are. I probably just worked harder and cared more. My secret to getting all A's is very simple. No matter what my professors asked me to do, I did *more than expected.* For example, if my math professor assigned problems 1, 3 and 5, I would do 1, **2**, 3, **4** *and* 5. If the history professor assigned us to read chapters one and two, I would read chapters one, two, and part of three. I wouldn't do *a whole lot more* than expected. But I would constantly and continuously do more than expected each and every day."

If you **DMTE**—**D**o **M**ore **T**han **E**xpected—it'll never fail you. Absolutely! Positively!! Guaranteed!!!

~It's not where you start, it is where you finish.~

■ ■ ■

CHAPTER 7

RESPONSE

"Life is not what happens to you.
It is how you respond to what happens to you.
Life is a series of problem-solving events."

~Dr. Rob Gilbert

The Magic
ACRONYMS, FORMULAS,
& IMPACTFUL STORIES
of Leadership

A Tribute to the Amazing Dr. Rob Gilbert
& the Success Hotline

THE LITTLE VOICE

by Rich Kennedy

Richard Kennedy was a student of Professor Robert Gilbert more than 30 years ago at Montclair State University. Richard was also a competitive ski racer for many years, earning numerous victories. He's the greatest downhill racer in Montclair State's history, as he became an All-American! He has also worked in the legal industry for more than 30 years. Due to his long tenure as a Success Hotline caller, and with the ability to remind Dr. Gilbert of messages created long ago, Dr. Gilbert appointed him as the "Official Historian" of the Success Hotline.

▪

Shortly after I graduated, Dr. Gilbert established the Success Hotline, in which he created a new inspirational message every day—yes, *every day*! If you create the habit of calling the Success Hotline on a daily basis (OADB!), you will become aware of the *little voice* in your head. Everyone has that little voice. A habit starts as a thread and becomes a thick cable. The more you do it, the more you want to do it. Don't treat calling the Hotline as a job; treat it as a little dose of Vitamin E+ (Enthusiasm). Take a chance, and start to build the cable. Listen to *the little voice* right now as you are reading this: What is it saying to you?

The little voice can become your friend or foe; it is there whether you like it or not. Untrained, the little voice is primarily your negative foe. It may say things like this to you:

"I can't do this."
"I am too tired."
"I don't feel like it."
"It is raining out."
"It is too cold out."

It is easy for that little voice to convince you not to do something; however, by listening to the daily messages on the Success Hotline, the little voice in your head will soon start to become trained and become your friend. As the little voice starts to become trained as your friend, it may say this to you:

"I can do it."
"I have grit."
"I have moxie; a little rain, even a downpour, won't stop me."
"I don't mind the cold. I have a warm coat."
"I like going to the gym at 6:00 a.m. It's peaceful and energizing at the same time."

Once you train your little voice, it will become consistently more positive, and that type of good training becomes a powerful source for you. It will help you overcome and deal with problems, roadblocks, and speed bumps that pop up unexpectedly and are out of your control, yet they still happen. Be prepared for them, and you will be that much stronger at the end of each day. I like to check in on my little voice throughout the day. What is it doing and saying? You may notice that the voice never stops. If it gets off track during the day, a few positive affirmations can usually reset it in your favor.

"I feel great today."
"Today is a great day."
"I am unbeatable."
"I am energized."
"I am rejuvenated."

Those are a few examples of things I would do to get the little voice back on track. Make up your own affirmations, and come up with new ones. Life is constantly evolving; evolve with it. The more you do it, the better the feedback will be from the little voice. I like to do the affirmations, whether I think I need them or not; they are pushups for the brain, training that little voice.

It is a journey and challenge worth taking, and the Success Hotline is the roadmap to take you there. I have listened to more than 10,000 of the daily messages over the past 33 years, and I have never said, "Maybe I should stop listening to them now."

Good luck to you, and keep moving forward.

FROM THE SUCCESS HOTLINE ARCHIVES . . .

BXYKUZX WYACYCK

Dr. Rob: Stop. What are you thinking right now?

While reading that title, were you confused?

Did a little voice in your mind say something like, "What's this?" or "I'm confused!"?

First question: Do you realize there's a little voice in your mind?

When I ask you that question, if some little voice says, "There's no little voice up here," that's the little voice I'm talking about!

We all have a little voice in our minds that talks to us almost all the time.

This little voice can be your biggest fan or your biggest foe.

This little voice can encourage you or discourage you.

How would you talk to someone you wanted to inspire and motivate?

Maybe that's how to talk to yourself!

Maybe you should become your own best friend!

~If you can dream it, you can do it.~

~Walt Disney~

▪ ▪ ▪

CUP

I *have a stand-up table at school* that I *love*! It has cool, smooth rollerblade wheels, a sitting setting, and the obvious standing setting. There is a pen holder and a cup holder on the flat desk surface. I'm all set. Mobile, working, ready.

One morning, I was set to get started on my table, but the plastic cup holder was missing. Now, there was just a round hole in the table. *Maaaaaaaaan.* What the ____? Where could it have gone? Was someone testing me, busting my chops?

Days went by, no cup holder. Man, I was not happy. My perfect little table was now imperfect. This always happens to me. Who did this? Why did this happen? Complaining, complaining, complaining, till one morning—*Bam!* I was having my breakfast, and my yogurt cup slid right into it. And not like gently resting in the plastic cup holder, but like gravity-based, tight fit, like an adult trying to fit right through a kid-size round floatie—tight. I could sprint down the hallway, and that yogurt was not falling out. I had a new and improved cup holder—a different type that actually worked better. With a slight change in my coffee cup and in my water bottle, they fit now, sliding all the way through the table, tight!

So, what I didn't do was CUP—*Choose Ur Positive.* I was ticked about losing the plastic cup holder, but I never looked at the new type of cup holder I have. I did *not* "choose ur positive" or even try to find the positive. I just focused on the loss, not that this actually could be better.

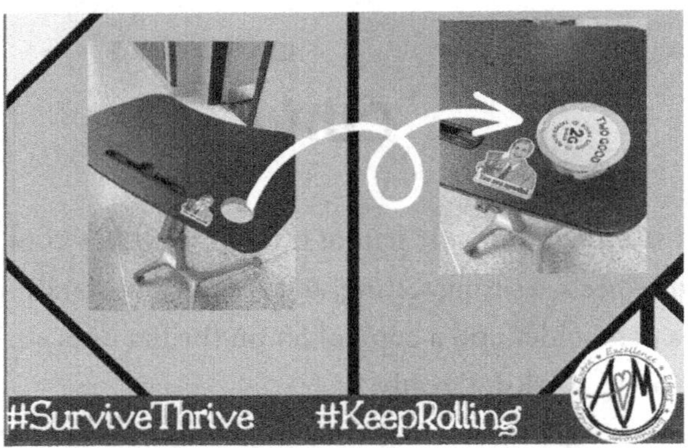

Dr. Gilbert consistently says on the Hotline, "Because of this, something good will happen!" This is an example. Also, I like this saying: "Things work out best for those who make the best of the way things work out."

In this simple and not serious situation, I did neither of these.

Life will constantly give us situations, good and bad, and we have a choice in how we *respond* to them. *CUP—Choose* ***Ur Positive.***

FROM THE SUCCESS HOTLINE ARCHIVES . . .

Who's Lucky???

Dr. Rob: It was Lucky's sixtieth birthday, and her husband threw a big party for the whole family in her honor.

Just before they brought out the birthday cake, one of their granddaughters asked Grandpa why everyone always called Grandma "Lucky."

"Oh, it's a nickname I gave Grandma right before we got married."

"Do you call her 'Lucky' because she really is lucky?" the child asked.

"Oh, I think Grandma definitely has her fair share of luck, but that's not why I called her that."

"Do you call her 'Lucky' because she brings you good luck?"

"I think Grandma sometimes brings me good luck, but that's not why I called her 'Lucky.'"

"I give up," she finally said, "What's the reason?"

Grandpa said, "I have always called Grandma 'Lucky' to remind myself how lucky I am to be married to her."

~Shoot for the moon. Even if you miss,
you'll be among the stars.~

■ ■ ■

THE BIRDCAGE

If you carry a birdcage around long enough, someone will give you a bird. Think about that statement. It's true, right? Let's play it out. You're walking around with that birdcage, and people will say things like, "Where are you going with that? Where is the bird? What type of bird do you have/want to get? Why don't you have a bird?" etc. They also will say things like, "Oh, my cousin owns a pet store," or "My mother is looking for a new home for hers," etc.

Dr. Gilbert is a master storyteller, and he also speaks in parables. *Well, this is one of them.* We are not actually speaking about birds. We are talking about that thing—that thing, that project, that job, that goal, etc.

In 2014, I had been calling Dr. Gilbert and the Success Hotline for a short while, but I never actually spoke to him. I had screwed up the toss at a game at Duke University on National television. I shared this story in Chapter 2 in the excerpt entitled "I can do this." It wasn't just any game at Duke—it happened to be the game that Coach K tied the all-time record for wins. You can read about it here: https://bit.ly/TalesTheToss.

This mistake was stuck in my head, and I developed a sort of mental block about tossing the ball. My body would stiffen up, and my arms and chest would tighten. Imagine trying to toss a ball in the air with a thick rope wrapped tightly around my arms and chest—that's what it felt like.

Someone said to me, "Why don't you talk to Gilbert? You know, you can leave him a message. *He will definitely help you.*"

Call and talk to a stranger about one of the most personal, embarrassing things that happened in a mega-public setting? Ahhh. . . . *No.*

I called for a few weeks, and then I did it. I asked Gilbert for help. I left a message telling him what had happened, and *Bam!* He called me! ***Dr. Gilbert put a bird in my birdcage*** and gave me some incredible solutions to my issue. It was perfect.

A second example was writing these books. When I started, I can't tell you how many people offered help and advice as I started my journey. Incredible education leaders like Todd Whitaker, Jimmy Casas, Joe Sanfelippo, Tom Murray, and others had conversations, zooms, coffee, and a beer, and I absorbed all their advice. Many times, all you have to do is ask!

Now that I have been blessed in learning how to write books, I offer free book seminars to any and all who want to attend. You can view them here: https://bit.ly/AMWriteMyBook

Put yourself, your birdcage, and what you want to do *out there*. People will help you. They want to help you, so put the birdcage out there!

FROM THE SUCCESS HOTLINE ARCHIVES . . .

"Nature abhors a vacuum."

~Knowledge minus action = zero.~

▪ ▪ ▪

FAIL

by Dr. Hal Abraham

Dr. Hal Abraham is an accomplished superintendent of schools, an adjunct professor at Montclair State University, and a former student-athlete at MSU. He attributes much of his success to the teaching and mentorship of Dr. Gilbert.

▪

As ***a former student-athlete*** under Dr. Rob Gilbert's guidance at Montclair State University and now a school administrator in New Jersey, I consistently draw upon the profound impact and teachings of Professor Gilbert. His mentorship has become a touchstone, shaping my approach to education and leadership. I frequently share my experiences with Dr. Gilbert as a compelling example of the transformative influence a passionate educator can wield, not only on individual lives but also on the broader world. Dr. Gilbert's teachings continue to resonate, serving as a reminder of the enduring power of dedicated mentorship and the ripple effect it can have on shaping future leaders and making a positive impact on the world.

Dr. Gilbert's emphasis on the importance of time management, grit, and the transformative impact educators can have on individuals' lives has been a cornerstone of my approach as a school administrator. He demonstrated on a daily basis that, to be a true difference-maker, one must go above and beyond to make the learning experience both enjoyable and memorable.

Among the many memorable lessons, one stands out prominently—the acronym FAIL, which Dr. Gilbert aptly described as the "***First Attempt In Learning.***" His insistence that *failure is an integral part of the learning process* resonated deeply with me. It taught my colleagues and me that some may quit after encountering setbacks but that those who persevere and work diligently are ultimately met with success and an even greater skill set. This may be the single most important lesson a person can learn in life, and his style of teaching made this abundantly clear.

I vividly recall Dr. Gilbert's unique final-exam policy, allowing us to retake it as many times as necessary until we achieved the desired grade. This policy showcased his commitment to fostering a growth mindset and encouraging determination. I personally took advantage of this opportunity, retaking the final exam three times, even with one of the testing dates falling on New Year's Day. This approach alone demonstrated Dr. Gilbert's unique approach to testing and, more importantly, his genuine care for his students' growth.

As an educator, embracing a creative mindset and infusing a sense of joy into the learning process are essential components of fostering a dynamic and effective educational environment. Understanding that failure is an integral part of the learning journey is paramount; it not only demonstrates resilience but also serves as a powerful indicator of growth. Often, the most profound lessons emerge from moments of temporary setbacks, reinforcing the notion that *learning is a continuous and evolving process.* By encouraging a positive attitude toward failure, we create a supportive atmosphere, where students can develop a genuine love for learning, understand the value of perseverance, and, ultimately, grasp the essence of their greatest lessons.

Embracing failure is not a setback but rather a steppingstone to personal and professional growth. With the right mindset, failure transforms into a powerful catalyst, propelling us to new heights. It offers invaluable lessons, cultivates resilience, and fuels the determination needed to overcome obstacles. When viewed through the lens of learning, failure becomes an essential component of success, an opportunity to refine strategies, and a pathway toward achieving one's full potential. So, let us live by Dr. Gilbert's words and not fear failure. Instead, we should aim to change the world while understanding that it's okay to FAIL along the way!

FROM THE SUCCESS HOTLINE ARCHIVES . . .

The Hall of Fame of Temporary Failures

I've missed more than 9,000 shots in my career. I've lost almost 300 games. Twenty-six times I've been trusted to take the game-winning shot and missed. I've failed over and over again in my life. And that is why I succeed.

~Michael Jordan

Dr. Rob: Two guarantees about achieving success:

1. *It will be difficult.*
2. *It will be worth it!*

Part of the difficulty is that success is not easy. It's not supposed to be easy. You're always being tested. You might fail—but make sure that none of your failures are permanent. All failures must be temporary.

Permanent failure: "I can't do it."

Temporary failure: "I can't do it *yet*."

Right now is the perfect time to start practicing "the art of temporary failure."

Here's the Hall of Fame of Famous Temporary Failures.

Norma Jean Baker. In 1944, the director of a modeling agency told Norma Jean, "You'd better get secretarial work or get married." Norma Jean later changed her name to Marilyn Monroe.

Lucille Ball. In 1927, the head instructor of the John Murray Anderson Drama School suggested that she "try any other profession."

The Beatles. "Groups with guitars are on their way out" was the reason that Decca Records gave for rejecting The Beatles in 1962.

Albert Einstein. Believe it or not, this great physicist failed his first college-entrance exam at Zurich Polytechnic.

Michael Jordan. Pro basketball's greatest superstar was cut from his high school's varsity basketball team when he was in the tenth grade.

General Douglas MacArthur. MacArthur was rejected by West Point twice but was accepted the third time he applied.

Mickey Mantle. This Yankee Hall of Famer was never voted as "most athletic" in his high school.

Sidney Poitier. After his first audition, this future Academy Award-winner was told by the casting director, "Why don't you stop wasting people's time and go out and become a dishwasher or something?"

Elvis Presley. This superstar singer couldn't make his high school glee club. After Elvis's first performance at the Grand Ol' Opry on October 2, 1954, Opry manager Jim Denny told him, "You ain't going nowhere, son. You ought to go back to driving a truck."

Charles Schulz. The creator of "Peanuts" could not get his cartoons accepted by his high school yearbook.

All of these "Hall of Famers" experienced failure, but they all bounced right back. You'll fail, too. As a matter of fact, you want to fail. If you don't fail, it's because you're playing it too safe. If you don't fail, it's because you're not leaving your comfort zone. Fail, but bounce back. Fail, but be resilient. Master the art of *temporary failure.*

~I skate to where the puck is going to be, not where it's been.~

~Wayne Gretzky~

■ ■ ■

MBG–MBB

T*here was a farmer* in Eastern Oregon named George. One day, when George woke up, he saw that the door to his horse pen was broken open and that his one horse was gone! George was upset. He went into town to gather his supplies; the locals had already heard about George's misfortune. They questioned him, "George, how are you going to run your farm with no horse? What are you going to do?" George said calmly, "This might be good; it might be bad. You never know."

The next morning, George awoke to pleasantly find *three horses* in his pen. His own horse had returned, along with two others. He went into town again, his morning ritual, and the townsfolk once again commented on George's situation. "Wow, you're so lucky," they said. "You've now got three horses. That is incredible!"

George, again, calmly stated, "This might be good; it might be bad. You never know."

The next day, George's son was riding one of the new horses, trying to train her, and she bucked hard, throwing George's son from the horse, breaking his leg. George was quite upset about the injury, and when he headed into town, he heard all about it. "George, that is terrible news about your son. How are you going to run your farm without your son? What are you going to do?"

You could guess George's answer: "This might be good; it might be bad. You never know." The next day, the US Army knocked on George's door, recruiting young men into the draft for the war. They pronounced: "George, produce your son. He is to join us for the war." George calmly turned and showed his son, lying on the couch with his foot in the air and politely said, "Sorry, men—I don't think he will be able to join you."

Things work out best for those who make the best of how things work out. Never get too high. Never get too low. The reality lies somewhere right in the middle. George did not adopt the "woe-is-me" mentality or "the world is against me" mentality. He kept his cool, he stayed positive, and good things worked out through the bad. **MBG-MBB**

FROM THE SUCCESS HOTLINE ARCHIVES . . .

Problem Solving Made Easier

Dr. Rob: Life is a continuous series of problem-solving events. In most cases, our problems are not the problem—how we *handle* the problems is. The problem itself is the little problem. How you handle it is the big problem.

How do you handle your problems? Do you get fascinated or frustrated? Problems get easier with fascination.

They get more difficult with frustration. Problems get solved with fascination. Problems get more problematic with frustration.

Fascination brings energy. Frustration depletes it.

Thomas Edison was once asked how he dealt with the 12,000 failures he had before he invented the light bulb. Edison replied that he didn't fail 12,000 times; he *learned* 12,000 ways how not to invent the light bulb. Edison didn't experience the *frustration* of failure but the *fascination* of feedback.

Frustration never works. Fascination always does.

Fascination or frustration: Your choice.

~Pain is temporary. The pride is forever.~

■ ■ ■

FEAR: FALSE EVIDENCE, APPEARING REAL

There ***are many strategies***, techniques, and ways of doing things to move you forward in this book. There are things to equip you to have a positive mindset. This acronym is not one of those, but something that we do that holds us back. We make up our minds ahead of time or create situations that just aren't true. We might be angry about something or think that somebody doesn't like us because they didn't return a call or an email, and we make a story up in our mind. We create false evidence that appears to be real fear.

Why do we do this? Is this something that you've done in the past? I know fear has bitten me before when something happens. An example might be you do not get selected for a position. You think there's a negative reason why you haven't been selected yet—maybe they forgot to return your email. Maybe they picked somebody else they believed was a better person for the job or a better fit.

Replace the acronym FEAR with the mindset of the 5-SWs in Chapter 8. Sometimes it will; sometimes it won't—so what? Someone's waiting, so stick with it. Let's not create things in our minds or hearts that aren't true.

When you know the facts of the situation or have been given all the evidence, *then* you can form your opinions—but don't make them up based on circumstances that may or may not be true. This is something that can hold you back, so take "fear" out of your life and insert the five SWs when things don't go your way. Keep moving forward, and find another route. There's no *roadblock* out there, only *bends in the road* or *hurdles.* Find a way around them or above them, and keep moving forward.

FROM THE SUCCESS HOTLINE ARCHIVES . . .

The Real Culprit

Dr. Rob: Les Brown, the great motivational speaker, said: "The doctor's prognosis kills more people than the disease." What we think and believe is very powerful. According to legend, one day, a man was walking in the desert, where he met Fear and Plague. The man asked the two friends where they were going. They said they were on the way to kill an entire city of 10,000 people.

The man asked Plague, "Do you do it all by yourself?"

"Oh, no! That's too much work for me," Plague said.

The man was confused. Plague continued, "I'll just take care of a few hundred people, and then I'll let my friend Fear do the rest!"

~Your mind is like a parachute.
It works only when it is open.~

■ ■ ■

E + R = O

Event plus ______ equals outcome? What is that "R"? We all have so many events that happen in our lives: good, bad, crazy, etc. They happen. I used to think they happened only to me, and I had a "woe-is-me" mentality. I often question, "*Why does this happen to me?*" Especially working in schools, I was always on edge about these potential events: fights, drugs, bad social media posts, tragic incidents, and so on. I worked hard to prevent them, but they happened, and I wanted a good, peaceful outcome. I wanted an outcome in which I did not get ripped in public at a school board meeting or on the dreaded "Parent Facebook Group."

As I got older, and as I listened to the Hotline, I learned that it is the "R" that I should focus on. The "E's" happen everywhere and all the time. It is the "R" that has the biggest impact on what the outcome will be. **RESPONSE.** That's right, the *response*. How we respond to these incidents or events is crucial. They happen. They are embarrassing, sometimes hurtful, insulting, and more.

Here is an example of the E + R = O. In the late fall of 2022, I was in my 18th year as a building leader in the great school district, Port Jervis Schools, in the beautiful small city of Port Jervis, New York. At the time, I was the middle school principal, and we'd had an unfortunate string of negative events involving knives. Kids were posturing and trying to out-tough one another by bringing knives to school. No one whipped them out or used them, but they were caught possessing them—one knife, two knives, three, and so on.

We continued to follow the code of conduct regarding disciplinary consequences with these knives. We spoke to the students, sent out safety memos to staff, and so on. Then January came. We confiscated four in one week. *Four!*

I felt mounting pressure to do something and share this bad news, yet I cringed thinking about it. As written earlier, we think about the "E's"—the events—and are concerned about public backlash. I knew this was too much.

I met with the district leadership team, and I drafted this memo in conjunction with a school-wide phone call home to parents and staff: https://bit.ly/PJMSsafety

It was a Friday, and I braced for an onslaught of negative online social media posts, weekend voicemails from angry parents and concerned community citizens, and a loaded email inbox with parents demanding answers and action.

None of that happened. **None.** I actually got one voicemail *thanking* me for the information, and two emails also thanking me for working hard to keep our schools and the kids safe. ***E*** + ***R*** = ***O.*** Event plus response equals outcome. In this "event," I was very pleased with the outcome, proud of my school district, and happy that my response was transparent, timely, accurate, and direct, including the action steps taken (response). Things don't always work out this well, but, in this incident, they *did*, including no more knives for the remainder of the school year.

FROM THE SUCCESS HOTLINE ARCHIVES . . .

"You are 100% responsible for how you choose to respond to everything that happens in your life."

~A leader is one who knows the way, goes the way, and shows the way.~

■ ■ ■

CHAPTER 8

RESILIENCY

*"I am not judged by the number of times I fail,
but by the number of times I succeed; and the number of times
I succeed is in direct proportion to the number of times
I fail and keep on trying."*

~Tom Hopkins, sales trainer and author

The Magic
**ACRONYMS, FORMULAS,
& IMPACTFUL STORIES**
of Leadership

A Tribute to the Amazing Dr. Rob Gilbert
& the Success Hotline

WIT

by Karin Abarbanel

Karin Abarbanel is an author, playwright, and entrepreneur. Her nonfiction has been published by Penguin Random House, Henry Holt, and McGraw-Hill. She listens to Dr. Rob Gilbert's Hotline every day and credits it with much of her recent success!

▪

T***here was a time*** when a rejection or setback on a creative project would completely deflate me. I'd retreat, launch a new project, and slink away again when I encountered another obstacle. But Dr. Rob Gilbert's marvelous Success Hotline changed all this! I've been a devoted caller for more than 15 years (weekends included!), and Dr. Gilbert's action-packed tips have definitely strengthened my resiliency muscle and completely altered my attitude toward adversity. In fact, they've been life-changing.

I was so excited by their positive effect on me that I interviewed Dr. Gilbert as a motivational expert for ***Birthing the Elephant***, my start-up guide for women entrepreneurs. His Hotline also directly inspired me to launch karinwritesdangerously.com, my daily motivational blog for writers, with the goal of encouraging kindred spirits on the writing path, just as Dr. Gilbert has uplifted me and countless other callers.

Day by day, the Success Hotline spurs me to aim higher and push myself further as a writer. Of all Dr. Gilbert's messages and mantras, the one that has consistently helped me the most is "WIT:

Whatever **I**t **T**akes!" Combining it with two other action phrases—"Be Extreme!" and "Go All Out—Don't Hold Back!" gives me a trio of tools I can apply to fight through obstacles, push past self-imposed limitations, and often even surprise and surpass myself.

Just one example. Soon after 9/11, I felt compelled to write a long essay called, "September 11, 1776" about the dangers and hardships George Washington faced at the start of the American Revolution. Some years after the attack, I submitted it to a few magazines without success. Recently, as a major anniversary loomed, I committed to finally getting my essay published. It was a story of hope and resilience, and I felt it could uplift and comfort people during a dispiriting time.

This was a major challenge—long essays are very difficult to get into print. To help me stay focused and positive during the rejections I knew I'd face, I relied on WIT: *__W__hatever __I__t __T__akes, Be Extreme,* and *Go All Out.* For three days, I did nothing but identify potential outlets, chase down editors' emails, and tackle my targets. I canvassed my contacts for leads at *The New York Times, Newsweek*, and elsewhere. I enlisted a marketing pro to help me craft a compelling query letter and sent it out nonstop. Hour after hour, I queried *O Magazine*, *Esquire*, *The Guardian*, the *Saturday Evening Post,* and even *Vogue*, which sometimes printed long stories. I asked social media-savvy friends for online outlets. In all, I contacted more than 25 print and digital publications before I got a "Yes." Ultimately, *American Heritage* published my story in full, along with beautiful illustrations, in a special 9/11 online edition. What a thrill it was to see it! What a triumph over rejection!

Without WIT to spur me on, I would probably have quit after my 5th or 6th rejection—10 at the max. But WIT kept me going until the mission I committed myself to was accomplished. That's why I've used it again and again to fight through challenges. WIT wins out over obstacles and circumstances.

WIT reminds me that everything starts with me—success depends on my intention and energy. WIT also reminds me that *I'm* the master of my attitude and effort. Most of all, WIT simplifies everything for me. I just keep going, no matter what, coming up with new ideas and acting on them until I reach my goal.

FROM THE SUCCESS HOTLINE ARCHIVES . . .

"Success is the ability to go from one failure to another with no loss of enthusiasm."

~Winston Churchill, British Prime Minister

Often at the Success Hotline Zoom seminars, Karin would tell the following two stories . . .

JOHN KENNETH GALBRAITH

Harvard University professor John Kenneth Galbraith was one of the most famous economists of all time. He also published an incredible number of books and articles.

Shortly before Professor Galbraith died, a journalist asked him what he had learned from a lifetime of writing.

The professor responded, "The one most important thing I learned was that the quality of writing I did on the days I *didn't* feel like it was just as good as the quality of the writing I did on the days I *did* feel like it!"

The lesson here is professionals do the best when they feel like it least!

SINCLAIR LEWIS

Many years ago, Nobel Prize-winning novelist Sinclair Lewis was scheduled to give an all-day seminar for college students, on writing. Lewis began the seminar with a question: "How many of you really intend to be writers?" *Every single student* in that room raised a hand.

After slowly looking around the room, Lewis packed up his briefcase and said, "In that case, my most important advice to you is to go home and write." And, with that, the great Sinclair Lewis left!

This famous writer knew the secret. You can *think* about writing, you can *talk* about writing, you can *attend seminars on* writing, but if you really want to be a writer—you have to *write*.

Very simply—writers write.

~If it is to be, it is up to me.~

▪ ▪ ▪

NO

NO—***you didn't get the job.*** *NO*—she/he doesn't want to date you. *NO*—you didn't win. Now what? *Next opportunity.* When you have this mindset, you are a winner. Dr. Gilbert often says that winners lose more than losers lose, and this includes "being told *NO*." You will be told *NO* more in your life than you are told *Yes.*

Gilbert says, "It is not the number of times you are told '*NO*' that matters—it is the number of times you are told 'Yes.' The number of 'Yesses' you get is directly related to the number of times you are told *NO* and keep on trying. The point of it all: *NO* stands for *next opportunity.*

This is the story of someone I hired once; we'll call him "Mike." Mike was not my initial selection. I hired someone else. Mike was extremely grateful and thankful for the opportunity when I told him he did *not* get the job. I liked him, but he was not my pick.

The next day, I called him and asked if he'd be interested in a per diem substitute position. This is not a full-time teaching position but basically a substitute position, and you are guaranteed to work each day.

NO—Next opportunity. Mike said he'd love to. Mike started right away and was amazing. Energizing, positive, showing love and respect to the kids, and more. Just great! The guy I selected turned out to be a disaster—really, really bad, with several issues in just a few weeks. Who hired this guy again? I had to let him go ASAP.

Who did I turn to as a quick fix and immediately hire? You guessed it: *Mike!* That's correct. Mike, who was initially told *NO* and took the *next opportunity* with grace and gratitude, slipped right into the job. Do you think he was great when he got the full-time job? Heck, yeah! Mike is a great example of making the best of *NO* and moving on to your next opportunity. You will be/have been told *NO* many times on your journey: "It is how you show up afterward that really will make the difference." Show up awesome. Show up as Mike did.

Show up like Mike Piazza and Tom Brady did, both Hall of Famers in their sport (baseball and football). Dr. Gilbert always likes to share where they were drafted into the pros: Piazza: 1,390th in the 62nd round! *Wow!* You talk about the *next opportunity*! There were 1,389 people who got an opportunity before Piazza, and those teams essentially told him *NO*. Brady—very similar: 199th in the 6th round of the NFL draft.

These two are more examples of *NO*—**N**ext **O**pportunity. They certainly made the best of their opportunities. Nobody cared what number they were drafted at or that Mike wasn't my first selection. It was the job they did and how they showed up that people cared about, and it made the difference in their careers.

FROM THE SUCCESS HOTLINE ARCHIVES . . .

Shake It Off and Step Up!

Dr. Rob: One day on a ranch, a baby donkey asked Grandpa, "How can I grow up to be big and strong like you?"

"That's simple," said the elder donkey. "You just have to learn how to do two things: shake it off, and step up."

Then Grandpa told this story: Once upon a time, a donkey fell into a well. The farmers came by, saw what had happened, and discussed what to do. They decided that getting the donkey out of the well was not worth the trouble, and they didn't want anyone to fall in, so they began to fill the shaft with dirt.

Each time a shovelful came down, the donkey shook it off and stepped up. The farmers kept shoveling, the donkey kept shaking, and they kept shoveling and the donkey kept stepping up. Sure enough, the farmers soon filled the well! They filled it to the brim, so the donkey was able to step right out and never worry about falling back in!

You're going to have dirt shoveled on you every day in the form of gossip, criticism, negative comments. This won't come only from the outside but from the inside as well. Your biggest critic might be yourself. Your biggest demotivator might be yourself. No matter where the dirt comes from, you've got to be as smart as a donkey. Instead of letting the dirt bury you, just shake it off, and step up.

There's no guarantee that the critics will ever stop shoveling, but if you keep shaking it off and stepping up, it won't matter.

~Be consistently persistent.~

▪ ▪ ▪

A WAVE DOESN'T CRASH WHERE IT STARTS

I've always enjoyed the ocean. I once took a trip with my wife to Costa Rica, and *wow*—such beautiful, long waves. Deep, long beaches, where the waves started forming far out and continued to roll in. Many surfers enjoy this area due to this phenomenon. They were not a roll-and-crash type of waves, like you see on most beaches, yet long, rolling flat waves—that just seemed to keep going and going.

A wave doesn't crash where it starts. I often reflect on my life now: where I am, where I'm going, where I want to be, and where I've come from. My wave is constantly churning, burning, and rolling. I love saying, "Keep rolling, friends," which I borrowed from my friend Dan Spainhour.

What is that wave for you? What is it that you are working on or trying to get to? While there may be complex, more challenging components to what you are doing, I challenge you to put two simple steps in place for your wave: **#1. *Start* and #2. *Keep rolling***, keep going, keep at it, and keep showing up. It's Dr. Gilbert's mantra: *Don't quit. Can't fail.*

Let's use the example of trying to lose weight and/or eating healthier. You step up on the scale and see a number you don't like. We've all been there. This year, at my annual physical, I was ten pounds heavier than I was the year before. *Yikes. Ten pounds!* I felt terrible. Man, what was I to do? A wave doesn't crash where it starts.

I've been active since I was a child—running around, playing, hooping, and more. I am still active, yet I don't burn calories or process food like I used to. It was time for a change. I started counting calories for the first time in my life. I tried different trackers and systems. I started reading the labels more carefully and just tracked the calories. 2100 was the number assigned by the doctor. *Keep rolling. Just start and keep rolling.*

I actually enjoyed the process. Was it perfect? No. Did I go over some days? Yes, buffalo pizza and cold beer on Friday nights are not the best habits! Yet it goes back to starting and keep doing that habit. **K**eep **o**n **k**eeping **o**n—KOKO—as Dr. Gilbert says. *A wave doesn't crash where it starts.* Since starting, I've lost ten pounds and set a goal for the weight I want to get to and maintain. I write down the calories, work toward those 10,000 steps, and keep rolling.

In 2024, I created a challenge coin for myself and for people I look to inspire/who are looking to be inspired. I think the concept of the *Waves* and *Keep Rolling* gives people hope. Good things will happen if they keep showing up and doing what they are trying to accomplish—or becoming the person they are working to be.

So, what is your plan? Get organized, get focused, and START—Your wave is just starting.

FROM THE SUCCESS HOTLINE ARCHIVES . . .

Dr. Rob: Sarasate, the great Spanish violinist of the 19th century, was once called a "genius" by a famous critic. Upon hearing this, Sarasate shook his head and said, "Genius! For 37 years, I've practiced 14 hours a day, and now they call me a 'genius.'"

KOKO is an acronym that stands for **K**eep **O**n **K**eeping **O**n.

GOYA—stands for **G**et **O**ff of **Y**our **A**natomy—and refers to getting it going. **KOKO** refers to keeping it going.

QUESTION: How long do you have to Keep On Keeping On?

ANSWER: Until you get what you want! Until you get your Rhodes Scholarship! Until you make it to Broadway! Until you write your best-selling novel. Until *you* do the impossible!!!

And you have to Keep On Keeping On, *no matter what* gets in your way.

~What could you achieve if you acted as if it were impossible to fail?~

■ ■ ■

VELCRO

Be like Velcro. Dr. Rob has taught me many things over the years. One thing, when publicly speaking, was to relate to your audience and use props. I have been a Secondary Principal for 21 years in the great small city of Port Jervis, New York. This was during the era of the birth of cell phones in teenagers' hands (and minds) in schools and on social media. We went through a lot of growing pains during this time, and the kids learned the good and bad of the power of their words and actions on social media and texting. Much of it was dumped on school administrators and teachers.

When we grew up (the adults) and went home over the weekend or Tuesday night, a kid couldn't comment to us because they were not in our vicinity. They would have to pick up their house phone and call us. There was no electronic communication, such as email, texting, or apps. Good "old-fashioned" talking. So, while kids still said mean things to others, we just dealt with it, and eventually, it just faded away.

A post, picture, or text can be very damaging to a young person and even adults. They can stare at it and read it over and over. It can go away if they hit that ever-powerful "delete" or "block" button, but many folks can't. It's like driving by a bad car wreck; you just can't take your eyes off it.

I began encouraging kids to delete and block others and *be like Velcro*. I would actually cut small pieces of Velcro and have kids put them in their pockets to remember the point. When I speak to groups of kids at assemblies, I demonstrate the point of the prop: You can choose if the comment, good or bad, sticks.

So, take two opposite pieces of Velcro: one has the tiny hooks, and the other has the tiny loops. Put them together, and *Bam!* Stuck together tight. That is how it works. If you flip one piece of Velcro over, the parts will *not* connect. You can choose to do that. You can choose the content, the words you want to absorb. You don't have to stick to everything.

Not only does this work for kids at school—it works for adults, too. It is a *choice of how we respond*. We do get to choose. Sometimes, we make excuses: "I lost my temper," or "I just couldn't help myself." Looking at it like two pieces of Velcro is as simple as turning over that piece of velcro to the other side.

Try it. Keep two pieces on your desk or somewhere you are often. When something upsets you, flip the pieces over, so that the hooks and loops are *not* touching. You can choose not to absorb the situation or let it stick to you. Be like Velcro. Not everything has to stick to you. When you can let things go, it is much more freeing. Find something you are passionate about or that will lift your spirits. Then stick to that!

FROM THE SUCCESS HOTLINE ARCHIVES . . .

You Can Have It All!

Dr. Rob: No matter how bad things get in your life, I can guarantee one thing: You can still have it all! If you do one thing: *Do not give up on yourself.* Keep showing up at school, keep showing up at work, keep auditioning, keep writing. If you don't quit, I can absolutely guarantee that you will not fail. It might take a miracle, but miracles are happening all the time. Let me tell you about one . . .

Once upon a time, there was a blind man who was very poor. He lived in a tiny house with his wife. The couple wanted children, but they never had any. Even though the man faced a great many difficulties, he lived an exemplary life. He was a very good man.

One day an angel appeared at the man's door. The angel said, "You have very little, but you have shown great faith. Because of this, you will be granted one wish and only one wish. I will return tomorrow at this time to receive your wish." The man was stunned. When he told his wife what had happened, she said, "Ask for *sight*—then you will be able to see me and the rest of the world for the very first time. Ask for sight. It will be so exciting!"

The man knew he wanted sight, but he also knew he wouldn't be satisfied with "just sight" because *he wanted it all.* When he told his relatives what happened, they said, "Ask for children. They will be a source of joy forever. Ask for children. Having a young family will be so exciting!" The man knew he wanted children, but he also knew he wouldn't be satisfied with "just children" because *he wanted it all.*

When he told his friends what had happened, they said, "Ask for money. Money will buy you happiness. Ask for money. If you have riches, life will become so exciting!" The man knew he wanted money, but he also knew he wouldn't be satisfied with "just money" because *he wanted it all.*

He thought and thought and thought . . . The next day, the angel reappeared at his front door; the angel asked the man for his wish.

"I wish," he told the angel, *"I wish to see my children eating off of golden plates."*

The wish was granted. The man received everything he wanted. The man, his wife, and his family lived happily ever after.

~You are 100% responsible for how you choose to respond to everything that happens in your life.~

■ ■ ■

START, STOP, CONTINUE

C*onstantly looking, seeing, and checking* what's happening for you in your life. What are you looking to start, looking to stop doing, and where are you continuing on your journey? This is a process that should happen multiple times a year, like cleaning out the garage or cleaning that filter. Let's begin with the *start.* Dr. Gilbert has shared many times on the Hotline that *it is the start that stops most people.* **Turn one day into Day One!**

Start: *What is it?* That project, that vacation, that healthy habit. Carry around an index card with a pen for two straight days. When those thoughts pop into your head—"Oh, I'd like to do that" . . . or "I wish I . . ." What is that thing? Write it down on the card. After forty-eight hours, what do you have? What is on your list? Circle the top three things you *really* want to do. What are they? Now—it is time. It is time to do that thing—that thing you have been wanting to do. Star it, circle it, underline it, and, most importantly, put it on the calendar/schedule. Get started. Make the time to do it. Put multiple reminders, and like NIKE says, just do it. **Just start.**

As I am writing this book, I am working hard to be in and stay in shape. I started doing one-minute planks daily. The first day, I felt like I got shot in my midsection area. I was shaking like a food mixer. I fell, swayed, staggered, and one minute felt like a year. Now, before I am done with the first few breaths, one minute has passed without me even looking at the clock. I work on my breathing, have some silent thought time, open my mind for gratitude thoughts, and more. Crazy, right? I am up to two minutes + each day now and counting. The start—*start* that thing. Just do it.

Stop: What is hurting you or unhealthy for you? What is it? Same process. Get that card again, and carry it around again for twenty-four to forty-eight hours. What is on your list? Now, a little different. Only *one* thing. Just circle *one* thing. What is the one thing that you *really* want to stop? *Really!* Then mark it down, and do it. Willpower, commitment, focus, discipline, and more. Do that thing. *I* know you can. *You* know you can. *Do it.* You are strong enough, powerful enough, and have the strength to do so. *Don't quit, can't fail.* You got this.

Lastly, this one is easy. You are already doing it/them. What are you doing that makes you want to continue? Getting up at 5 a.m.? Eating healthfully? Run streak? Reading daily? Working on that project each day? Saving money? Deposits consistently in the lives of others? *Keep rolling and keep going.* Thank you for your discipline and positive habits to keep doing the thing that you want to continue with. As Dr. Gilbert has said many times on the Hotline: A year from today, you will have wished that you started today. Continue on your journey. Life is a marathon, not a sprint.

FROM THE SUCCESS HOTLINE ARCHIVES . . .

Your Most Important Purchase

Dr. Rob: If you really want to be a champion, Milt Campbell, the great Olympic decathlon gold medalist, has three questions for you:

1. *Do you have goals?*
2. *Are your goals written down?*
3. *Are your written goals in your pocket right now?*

Why do this? You know what Coca Cola is. But, every day, you'll find Coke ads on TV, radio, the internet, and in newspapers and magazines. Coca Cola knows that, if you get constant and continuous reminders, eventually you'll buy Coke. It's called advertising. If it works for Coke—it'll work for you.

Milt Campbell knows this, too. Have your goals written on an index card in your pocket all the time. Read your goals, think about them, dream about them. Your written goals serve as constant and continuous reminders. Eventually, you'll buy your goals! You'll make them happen.

It's called advertising *for yourself.* It works for Coca Cola, and it'll work for you. It'll be the most important purchase you ever make!

~It's what you learn after you know it all that counts. ~

~John Wooden~

■ ■ ■

ACT DIFFERENTLY THAN YOU FEEL

"*But I am not confident.*" "*But I am not good at it.*" "*But I can't.*" "*But I don't feel like it.*" "*But I don't know how.*"

How many times have you said any of these statements? Countless, right? Coach Agresta coined the term *Act differently than you feel. Act as if* you *are* confident, and then you'll *become the way you act.* It is a choice to act differently than you feel.

I've heard so many superstars say how nervous they were when they first were "out there" on the big stage. I watched the *Beckham* documentary on Netflix. Soccer superstar David Beckham was really nervous in his first few "big" games, including his first World Cup. *Act as if.* So simple, yet so true.

Well, it feels fake. It feels like I am faking, to be someone I am not. I have often heard this sentiment expressed in my leadership talks around the country, when people share their thoughts on this topic—*that it just doesn't feel real. IT IS NOT SUPPOSED TO FEEL REAL*—that's why you can act differently than you feel.

I remember my first Assistant Principal job, outside Paterson, New Jersey, way back in 2004. It was an alternative school for kids who had been suspended from their day-school programs and sent to this alternative program at a different location. It was the first day, and I was standing at the door as the bus pulled up with the kids on it. Jacket and tie on (faking it, felt so uncomfortable), and my knees were shaking, almost buckling. I saw them saunter off the bus, headphones and hoodies on, heading toward me.

I took a deep breath, told myself, *"I can do this,"* over and over in my head, stuck my chest out and my shoulders up, and firmly and warmly said, "Good morning" to each student and instructed them to head to the auditorium for our initial meeting.

Hoooooooooooooooooooooooouuwwwwwwwwwwwww . . . I exhaled. I took another deep breath, was grateful I didn't fall down in front of the students, and told myself again, "I can do this." I walked into the auditorium with a smile, positivity, and enthusiasm, and off I went.

I acted differently than I felt. I didn't feel ready and was scared, but I acted as ready as I could be. And it worked. It worked each time until I really started to feel comfortable. Fast-forward one year, and I landed at my school for the next twenty-five years, Port Jervis Schools in Port Jervis, New York. I felt similar, yet not as bad. I was faking it and acting, again, until, a couple of weeks in, I started to get into a groove. It began to feel natural, and I started to feel more comfortable, more confident.

This pattern repeated itself when I became a father, started officiating college basketball, began speaking publicly, and so on. The *act as if* mantra has carried me through so many hard "first" times. Take it with you on your journey, too!

FROM THE SUCCESS HOTLINE ARCHIVES . . .

Dr. Rob: A great example of "acting differently than you feel" can be found in one of the most famous sales books of all time—*How I Raised Myself from Failure to Success in Selling*, by Frank Bettger. The first chapter of this book isn't about selling—it's about baseball!

Here's the story . . .

Way back in 1907, Bettger was cut from a minor-league baseball team because the manager said he was "lazy." The only job Bettger could get was with a team in New Haven, in the lowest levels of the minor leagues.

Bettger promised himself that no one would accuse him of being "lazy" ever again.

He couldn't hit, run, or throw any better, but he began to *play* better as soon as he acted more energetically and enthusiastically. *He acted differently than he felt.* This turned his career around, and he eventually made it to the major leagues, where he played for the St. Louis Cardinals.

After an injury forced his retirement, he took a job in sales. Once again, he was doing terribly until he realized what the problem was—he was lazy. He decided that no one would ever accuse him of being "lazy" ever again. He didn't know any more about the product or the customers, but he began to sell more as soon as he acted more energetically and enthusiastically. *He acted differently than he felt.*

He turned his career around, and he became a superstar salesman, sales trainer, motivational speaker, and author. Here's what Frank Bettger learned: *You have to do it, and then you'll feel like doing it. In other words, you can create your feelings through actions.*

~The will to win is not nearly as important as the will to prepare to win.~

▪ ▪ ▪

THE 5 SWs

T*here are so many favorites.* So many, yet this has to be in my top five (pun intended!). This magic formula has helped me countless times on my journey of leadership, and it can help you, too—when you doubt yourself, when you strike out, when you get let go, when you fall, and more.

Sometimes it **W**ill
Sometimes it **W**on't
So **W**hat?
Someone's **W**aiting
Stick **W**ith it

I have said these words so many times that they just roll off my tongue, and the worry rolls off my shoulders. *Sometimes it will, sometimes it won't. So what? Someone's waiting—stick with it!* We are on a journey of leadership, and *it is a marathon, not a sprint.* There are many ups and downs, twists, and turns. These are *not* roadblocks but rather bends made to go around. If you just stop, that will be the end of the road for you, not just a bend in the road.

I was a men's Division I college basketball referee for 20 years. I loved it. I loved the action, the speed of the game, the intensity—the whole thing. I was also fortunate to have officiated in the ACC (Atlantic Coast Conference) for seven of those twenty years, and wow, was *that* awesome. The ACC is arguably the best basketball conference in the country, with historic hoops programs like Duke, North Carolina, Notre Dame, and others.

The supervisor of officials retired during my tenure at the ACC, and a new supervisor was appointed. I was not in his line for the future, and my time in the ACC quickly came to an end (*sometimes it won't*). I was devastated, and it totally took the wind out of my sails. I continued refereeing, but my heart just wasn't in it like it was before.

I wrote my first book, *The Principal: Surviving & Thriving*, in 2016, and, over the next few years, I started to speak and do workshops for school leaders, while being a building principal and referee *(Someone's waiting)*. The book really took off, resonating with educators and leaders, as did my inspirational speaking *(Sometimes it will)*. I really liked the feedback I was getting from educators and the participants in my workshops, and I felt like I was making a positive impact on others. I loved refereeing, but I really wasn't making an impact on others. It was with the combination of me *not* continuing with the ACC and the growth of my speaking and writing that I changed course and began to pursue the "Andrew Marotta, Surviving & Thriving" inspiration work *(So what? Stick with it.)*. And I haven't looked back. It has been a great change—and one that I didn't see coming.

I share this story of the end of my officiating career and the beginning of my public speaking and writing career as a perfect example of the ***5 SWs.*** I had many ups and many downs on the journey, and, in the end, if you *stick with it,* things will work out! And who would have thought? To put the icing on the cake, I even wrote a leadership book based on stories and experiences from my time as an official, *Tales from the Hardwood*. I wish you the best. Keep rolling on your journey. Dr. Gilbert reminds us often: *Don't Quit, Can't Fail.*

~Nothing great was ever accomplished without enthusiasm.~

~Ralph Waldo Emerson~

FROM THE SUCCESS HOTLINE ARCHIVES . . .

The Best Success Hotline Thoughts on Persistence

"It's not the *end* of the road, it's just a *bend* in the road."
"Don't place a *period* where God has placed only a *comma*."
"A *setback* is a *setup* for a *comeback*."
~DR. WILLIE JOLLEY

"I will until . . ."
"Trying times are not the times to stop trying."
~RAY OWEN

"Going slowly does not prevent arriving."
~NIGERIAN PROVERB

"The world has a lot of starters but very few finishers."
"When all else fails . . . use persistence."
"I never tried quitting, and I never quit trying."
~DOLLY PARTON, ENTERTAINER

▪ ▪ ▪

IF YOU HAVE A BIG-ENOUGH REASON WHY, YOU'LL FIND THE HOW

by Jim Stroker

Jim Stroker is an incredible motivational speaker from New Jersey. Jim has presented around the country to thousands of audiences, sharing his story of inspiration and motivation. He is a husband, dad, and coach. He is a true example of "Because of this, something good will happen." I am so grateful for Jim sharing his family story with us. You can learn more at https://coachstroker.com/

▪

D*r. Rob Gilbert just happened to show up* at the right time, at the right place, with the right person enough times in my life to be a crucial part of saving our family from devastation.

My son and daughter, Jake and Ali, when Jake was four and Ali was two, were in a traumatic car accident. Jake sustained a traumatic head injury and was in a coma for 14 days, with his life on the line. Ali sustained a spinal stroke and became paralyzed from the chest down. In the world of stress, losing a child ranks extremely high. Both our children's lives were on the line.

Gilbert, in a serendipitous way, just at the right time, changed everything for our family. It was a cold, dark morning, pitch dark. I felt the weight of the world on my shoulders, and, as many of us sometimes feel, going up against this opponent in this life field was too much.

I was a coach and teacher at Ridgewood High School at the time, in the middle of the varsity football season, working as the defensive coordinator. We had gone up against many teams that overmatched us, but this Goliath-like challenge was almost unthinkable, unbearable, and even unfair to children. I was in my car at 5:15, and for some reason, I was told to dial that number again. I had dialed it many times, but I needed something that day. I needed *magic*. And so, I pushed those numbers 973-743-4690. My mentor, teacher, and North Star answered the phone and said, *"If there's a big enough reason* ***why****, you'll always find the* ***how****."*

It caught my attention. "You've reached Success Hotline, message number 8320. This is Dr. Rob Gilbert."

On this day, he shared this most powerful and impactful story on the Hotline: It took place way back in the early 1930s, and the Barnum & Bailey Circus was flourishing. The big top consisted of the main events—lions and tigers, trained elephants, clowns, and tightrope walkers. Out on the perimeter of this giant front-and-tent were what they called sideshows—unusual, interesting shows like the rubber man, the world's tallest woman, the barking child, and then the biggest hit: the world's strongest man.

The strong man had been there six years and done three events each day. It was the most popular because of the sign outside suggesting, "Win $20,000." In the early '30s, this was equivalent to more than $100,000 today. Thirty-eight people piled into the tent for the first show of the day. The strong man's assistant came out from behind the curtain and said, "I will now introduce to you the strongest man in the world, and he will do feats of strength to prove his prowess."

From behind the curtain walked the strong man—bald-headed, bursting at the biceps, barrel-chested, and with an intimidating look. He called out, "Bring me the phone book." The assistant walked out with a phone book. He took it over his head, held both edges, and then ripped it right in half. The audience was in awe. Then, he yelled out, "Bring me that railroad tie." His assistant dragged out this giant piece of lumber. He snatched it over his head, held it up high, and then crushed it over his bulging right quadriceps. The audience's mouths opened up. They couldn't believe it. Then he screamed out, "Bring me the nail," and she brought out this 13-inch galvanized nail. He stuck it between his teeth, bent it like rubber, and then, with one big bite, bit it right in half. The audience couldn't believe it.

And then he said, "For my final feat of strength, bring me the suitcase, bring me the lemon, and bring me the glass." The assistant walked out, put the large suitcase on the table, and then handed the strong man the lemon and the glass. He held the lemon up over the top of the glass; he flexed his arm and started to squeeze the lemon. As he squeezed, drop after drop fell into the glass. With one last burst of strength, he squeezed it, and one last drop of lemon juice went into the glass. He looked at his assistant and said, "Open the suitcase." She went over, flipped open the case, and revealed $100, $50, and $500 bills stacked upon each other, with a small sign on the top of the suitcase that said, "$20,000."

He looked at the suitcase and said, "That is my life savings. Anyone here that can squeeze one drop of lemon juice from the lemon, it's yours!" Hundreds of people walked up and attempted to win the $20,000, but no one ever could. He gazed at his audience, and, then, in the back row, a hand went up. It was the hand of a gray-haired, frail woman. As she put her hand up, she stood up with her walker, and in a soft voice said, "I can do that." The strong man smiled and started to laugh, and all the audience members turned. They saw this elderly woman, and they began to laugh. The woman started to walk forward with her walker, and then the laughter turned to howling. Even the strong man couldn't hold it back, but she kept walking.

She walked right up to that suitcase, stopped, and gazed into that suitcase. Then suddenly, she reached into her blouse, pulled out a locket, opened it up, and stared at it. She looked and looked and looked at that locket for at least a minute and a half. Then she closed it up, dropped it back into her blouse, took her walker, and walked toward that lemon. She picked it up, held the glass underneath, and closed her eyes. With her eyes closed, she held that lemon up and started to squeeze. As she squeezed, unlike others, the veins in her arm almost started to pierce through the skin. Her arm became the super arm as she squeezed and would not stop. She kept squeezing longer than anyone else had ever squeezed. Then, with one last burst of energy, a loud sound came out of her mouth. Then it happened: Not one drop, but two drops of lemon juice fell from the lemon. The strong man stood there, shocked, stunned, in disbelief. The only words that could come out of his mouth were, "How did you do that?"

She reached back into her blouse, pulled out her locket, opened it up, and said, "Sir, this is my grandson. He's nine years old. He has leukemia and will die at the end of the week."

"If there's a big enough reason ***why****, you will always find the* ***how****."*

Gilbert repeated, "If there's a big enough reason why, and the why is about people you love, you will always find the how."

It was like magic. Suddenly, all the fear, all the self-doubt, all the nervousness started to vanish, and I felt strong—stronger than ever—because I knew the way was clear.

Gilbert has said a lot of things and told a lot of stories to a lot of people on a lot of days, but, on that day, he changed my life, and then we changed the lives of those two little children, Jake and Ali.

I've visited Dr. Gilbert's class many times. He's kept an eye on them like a dad. He's offered story after story that's helped me flip the situation upside down, helped me control the controllables, and helped me look at things with a different perspective—a perspective of miracles and magic.

Jake was told he could not handle the rigors of public school. His brain injury had left him severely disabled, with the use of only one arm. Ali was in a wheelchair and would never walk again. One man consistently shared different stories of inspiration with our family, day in and day out. Not only did we listen—we took his messages to heart. We felt like this was the messenger from a bigger power, giving us the strength to do what we had to do.

Jake graduated from Fairleigh Dickinson with honors and was named Employee of the Year at Whole Foods. He was told he could not attend public school, but when they gave him a chance, something unexpected happened.

We're inspired by Rob Gilbert, never missing a day. We've all been inspired by Dr. Rob Gilbert—even when he didn't feel like it, even when it was difficult, he showed up for us every day. And then Jake took Gilbert's message and brought it into his own life. In 2,340 days, he had made it through Kindergarten and all the way to the end of his senior year without one single mess-up. *That's Gilbert's power.*

Ali was in a wheelchair, but Gilbert told us stories of flipping obstacles upside down, turning problems into possibilities, and looking at a setback as a setup for a comeback. He wanted us to reframe Ali's injury and look at it not as a threat but as a gift. We took that mindset and moved forward. Ali was the first wheelchair-bound actress to graduate from the Tisch School of Performing Arts at NYU. She appeared on *Glee* in her first TV hit and then, in 2015, became the first wheelchair-bound actress in the history of Broadway.

In 2019, she won a Tony Award for her role as Ado Annie in *Oklahoma!* She became the first Tony Award winner in a wheelchair in the 120-year history of the Tony Award. Gilbert has a lot of wins under his belt. He's changed a lot of lives. He's made people better through his incredible gift of saying the right thing at the right place to the right person. He did that for our family.

FROM THE SUCCESS HOTLINE ARCHIVES . . .

Dr. Rob: "There is absolutely nothing in the Success Hotline Archives that compares to or could possibly add to Jim's story.

I am totally humbled."

~There is only one game that truly counts—your life.
How will you respond?~

~Jim Stroker~

■ ■ ■

THE WHITE LINE

by Terrie Wurzbacher

Dr. Wurzbacher has studied under Dr. Gilbert since 2021. She credits Dr. Gilbert with helping her to finally to complete the 314-mile race across Tennessee unsupported.

Dr. Terrie spent 30 years on active duty in the Navy and then 16 more years working as a civilian for the Army. She was first an emergency room physician working in combat and disaster medicine; after a period of administrative responsibilities, she finished her Navy career in the Navy disability system. When she retired from the Navy, Dr. W went to work for the Army as a civilian—also in their disability system.

Since retirement, she enjoys doing ultra walking events, writing books, hosting a podcast, and now a daily call titled "Talking with Dr. Terrie—180 seconds to a Better You" Call today! 210-390-6100.

▪

T***raveling down the Tennessee country roads***, I could see only about fifty feet ahead, and all of that was *the white line.* It was the middle of the night, and I was exhausted, having had only three hours of sleep per twenty-four hours over the past eight days. I had been on my feet for twenty-one hours, desperately trying to cover the 314 miles in the required ten days. I dialed the phone, and the voice at the other end said, "What's up?" He didn't even sound as if I'd woken him up.

"I can't go on" were the words that fell out of my mouth. "Where are you? How do you feel? When can you rest again?" All his questions were meant to get me to think and not moan and groan about how crappy things were. I answered them all, but I still wanted to whine. He continued to volley questions, and then came the acronyms. I hate acronyms, by the way. I can never remember them. He was testing me.

"HOPE, Terrie—you know—**H**old **O**n, **P**ossibilities **E**xist."

"Sure, there's no hope," I mumbled, or maybe just thought.

We bantered back and forth until I screamed at him that I didn't want any more platitudes. "I can't do this!" I barked. He just let me vent, knowing that fatigue can destroy so much. He knew I was operating on fumes. But he also knew how to handle that.

"I'm going to ask for a crew. I can't make it 'screwed.'" I was almost in tears. Since 2014, I have been trying to finish this race across Tennessee unsupported, and every year, I have had to ask for a crew at some point. I had worked so hard this past year to deal with all the obstacles I encountered in 2021. Many were physical, but most were in the psychological realm—his realm. I had studied his work endlessly, along with everyone else I could find.

"Let's calm down and see what there is in front of you that you can control. Remember to focus on those things you can control, and let the others go." For some reason, that hit the spot, and I was able to concentrate on those things. I think it was because they were objective and didn't involve trying to put myself in some other mental state—a feat that was impossible in my current state.

"When can you rest again, even if it's not in a bed?" His calm, matter-of-fact voice seemed to ground me. I looked at my surroundings and told him what I thought. Next, he asked about my hydration and nutrition status—all objective things I could address. By then, I was feeling better, even though I was still exhausted. He had redirected my mind onto facts and tasks. He had also magically known to wait until all the stress hormones released by my desperation circulated through my system (only about ninety seconds), knowing that my body would recalibrate if he could just abort a repeat loop.

He finished off with, "Remember, Terrie, out of this, something good will happen!"

I quipped back at him, somewhat back to my "normal" self, "That's yours. For me, it's 'Everything always works out for Terrie!' But thank you for reminding me." I have believed that with all my heart and soul since 1985, and it has been true. I think that's one thing that has bonded us together. For those ten days in July 2022 (and again in 2023), Dr. Robert Gilbert used my experiences to illustrate his principles of success on his Success Hotline. Each day, he would distill the adventures of the previous twenty-four hours for the listeners. Since both years contained multiple obstacles, it was an excellent opportunity to teach while telling the story. There is no greater storyteller than Robert Gilbert!

Without his wisdom, concern, and his rallying the troops of the Success Hotline, I'm not sure I would have finished the Last Annual Volunteer State 500 K race (aka Vol State). It's 314 miles across Tennessee on country roads in the heat and humidity of July, carrying everything I needed for 10 days on my back. In the two years he's traveled along with me (virtually), I succeeded in finishing as the oldest woman to do so. It does take a village. But that village has to have a mayor, and **Dr. Robert Gilbert is the mayor of my village.**

FROM THE SUCCESS HOTLINE ARCHIVES . . .

Dr. Rob: In honor of the remarkable Dr. Terrie, who fills our July days with anticipation, upset, excitement, and most of all—AWE!

It is not the critic who counts; not the man who points out how the strong man stumbles, or where the doer of deeds could have done them better. The credit belongs to the man who is actually in the arena, whose face is marred by dust and sweat and blood; who strives valiantly; who errs, who comes short again and again, because there is no effort without error and shortcoming; but who does actually strive to do the deeds; who knows great enthusiasms, the great devotions; who spends himself in a worthy cause; who at the best knows in the end the triumph of high achievement, and who at the worst, if he fails, at least fails while daring greatly, so that his place shall never be with those cold and timid souls who know neither victory nor defeat.

~THEODORE ROOSEVELT (1858–1919) 26TH PRESIDENT OF THE UNITED STATES~

~Whether you think you can or you think you can't, either way, you are right.~

~HENRY FORD~

■ ■ ■

THE OBSTACLE IS THE WAY

I love this book by Matthew Kelly. It really refocused my thinking and mindset about issues, problems, and navigating difficult situations. *The Obstacle Is the Way.* Very simply put, this paradigm shift changed my thinking from *Why is this roadblock in my way? Why me? Why now?* to *This is supposed to happen* and *I just have to find a way around it.* This obstacle is just part of the process. It is closely related to Doc's "It is *not* the end of the road, but a *bend* in the road."

I used to think it was only me that these things would happen to. Not that perfect leader over there or that person who has it all together—*Why don't they have these types of issues? Why me?* It was on my leadership journey that I began to realize *that they* do *have these issues* and problems. They just learn to work around them. We all encounter them, yet what you do with the problem or roadblock makes all the difference.

Whatever field you're in—education, leadership, sales, athletics, etc.—Google your favorite performer, and read about their background. They have struggled! A few stories come to mind that Dr. Gilbert shared on the Hotline.

1. Scott Hamilton, Olympic figure skating champion. In an interview, Gilbert shared that Hamilton, throughout his practices over the years, fell more than 40,000 times! *40,000!* That is a few obstacles for sure, yet it is getting through those

obstacles, through those falls that is the real magic, the real secret. The falls are part of the success!

2. I vividly remember one time at the University of North Carolina, when I was officiating a college basketball game in the ACC. I made a terrible call against the home team, the North Carolina Tar Heels. I blew the whistle, made the call and associated signals, then, in like one second, I heard and felt a loud wave of boos. It literally smacked me in the back and neck like a wave in the ocean you didn't see coming—it was so loud and so strong. I looked over at my partner, who was a veteran in officiating. He had a huge smile and was quietly chuckling at my bad call. In so many ways, he was telling me, *Don't do that again!* And I learned right there from the obstacle: Don't make bad calls! Hold your whistle, see what you got, and make the correct calls. Blow the whistle when you're right!

3. The third story is a book—*Shoe Dog*—by Phil Knight, the owner and CEO of Nike. It's a great book with a ton of lessons. Phil shares many ups and downs on his journey of building his multi-billion-dollar company. *He started selling the shoes out of the back of his car at track meets!* Incredible, right?

Even just starting his journey and travels, Phil hit a major obstacle. He went to Asia for a series of business meetings with his partner and colleague. A few weeks into this business adventure, his partner met a woman, fell in love, and told Phil he was *not* continuing on with him on the trip. He was going to marry this woman and stay with her. *Wow!* This was long before the internet, cell phones, and other modern conveniences. Phil was a young kid in his 20s from Oregon. On his own. Oh, my.

He could have canceled his trip and gone home. It could have ended it right there, but no: *The obstacle is the way.* Phil did it. He continued on, super-focused on the meetings and the work to be done to grow Nike, and made it work. The whole story is that any journey is going to run into an "obstacle," a series of wins and failures, learning and growing on this journey. *Remember this on your journey: The obstacle is the way.*

FROM THE SUCCESS HOTLINE ARCHIVES . . .

Oldies but goodies: Life Changing Books

Dr. Rob: In March of 2009, I asked Success Hotline callers to tell me the books that changed their lives.

Here's that list . . .

- *Catcher in the Rye*—J.D. Salinger
- *Bad Childhood, Good Life*—Laura Schlessinger
- *The Seven Spiritual Laws of Success*—Deepak Chopra
- *Man's Search for Meaning*—Viktor Frankl
- *The Magic of Thinking Big*—David Schwartz
- *Psycho-Cybernetics*—Maxwell Maltz
- *The Secret of the Ages*—Robert Collier
- *The Tipping Point*—Malcolm Gladwell
- *Life 101*—Peter McWilliams
- *A New Earth*—Eckhart Tolle
- *The Last Lecture*—Randy Pausch
- *You're Hired*—Bill Rancic

- The entire *Harry Potter* series—J.K. Rowling
- *Tuesdays with Morrie*—Mitch Albom
- *Rich Dad, Poor Dad*—Robert Kiyosaki
- *Excuse Me, Your Life Is Waiting*—Lynn Grabhorn
- *Alcoholics Anonymous*—(the Big Book)
- *Think and Grow Rich*—Napoleon Hill
- *The Greatest Secret in the World*—Og Mandino
- *The Greatest Salesman in the World*—Og Mandino
- *Mastery*—George Leonard
- *A Return to Love*—Marianne Williamson
- *The Anatomy of the Spirit*—Carolyn Myss
- *How to Have Fun without Failing Out*—Rob Gilbert
- *What Color Is Your Parachute?*—Richard Bolles
- *Codependent No More*—Melanie Beattie
- *The Secret*—Rhonda Byrne
- *How I Raised Myself from Failure to Success in Selling*—Frank Bettger
- *How to Win Friends and Influence People*—Dale Carnegie
- *The Traveler's Gift*—Andy Andrews
- *Atomic Habits*—James Clear

~A year from today, you will wish you had started.~

▪ ▪ ▪

GOOD ENOUGH TO MOVE ON

Are you stuck because something's not perfect? Are you trying to make it better and keep going back to it time and time again? What project, book, lesson, or presentation are you working on but just can't let go? I have learned on my journey to get to a point where it is *good enough to move forward and move on.* Yes, I *want* it to be awesome. *Banging. Hot. Dope*—all of those and more, but I also have to keep moving. Sometimes, we drive ourselves crazy and keep going back over and over and over. Yes, you want to work at it and make it as great as possible, but enough is enough. Get it (that project, meal, presentation, etc.) to where it is good enough to move on. You have a lot to accomplish and get to on your journey. Don't fixate. Work hard, make things awesome, and keep moving. *Make it good enough to move on.*

One strategy to add to this is to *sleep on it.* Sleep on that project, and when you wake, you can tweak, change, and more. You will see from a new perspective and maybe a little bit from a different lens. Give it a try. This is freeing and allows you to let go and get moving. Life is short. Get it good, and keep moving.

A second strategy is to ask two or three trusted friends for some feedback. Ask them to be specific and give you a few constructive points of feedback. When they do, if you like the points, add them to your work, and then get moving. Submit it, turn it in, or give that presentation.

The last strategy you can try is a soft opening or release. Maybe put that "thing" out there, and see where it lands. If it's a presentation, try giving it to a small group first before presenting it to a larger audience. Comedians do this all the time. They try those new jokes on Tuesday and Wednesday before performing in the big arena on Friday night.

Country music stars pop into a small bar in Nashville on a random night to try out some new music, get a feel of the crowd, and get some feedback. They do it all the time. So can you! Get it to where it is good enough to move on.

FROM THE SUCCESS HOTLINE ARCHIVES . . .

Perfect is the enemy of good.

~VOLTAIRE, FRENCH WRITER AND PHILOSOPHER

■ ■ ■

MR. D'AMATO

D***r. Gilbert really loves this story.*** He has told it many times, usually during one of his streak weeks: Mr. D'Amato. Mr. D'Amato went to his doctor every year on his birthday. The doctor warmly greeted him, and then he did his checkup. He asked, "How old are you this year?"

Mr. D'Amato proudly exclaimed, "100 years old."

The doctor said, "Wow, Mr. D'Amato! You are in great shape. Better than last year! What is your secret?"

Mr. D'Amato simply stated, "I walk five miles every day."

"Every day?" the doctor asked.

"Yes, every day," Mr. D'Amato shared.

"That's great. Well done. What do you do when it rains?" the doctor asked.

"I put on a raincoat."

I put on a raincoat.

That is such a simple answer to such a roadblock for so many of us—the discipline to complete a task each and every day. *I put on a raincoat and walk the five miles.* There are so many tips related to this type of discipline in this book because it really *is* a mental challenge more than a physical challenge:

OADB, act differently than you feel, it's not what you are going through—it's where you are going to, the little voice, C > F = R, and so on. Doing that thing adds up each day, and the secret is *just doing it.* Mr. D'Amato just walks each and every day.

This story also makes me think about what I will be like when I am 100 years old. How am I going to feel? How am I going to look and sound? And can I walk five miles at 100 years old?? Well, I don't know the answers to those questions, but I *do* know that I have to start walking five miles a day *now*, not at ninety-five. *Habits start out like thin threads that turn into thick cables.* The more you do them, the stronger they become. Health habits and exercise habits are not a *sometimes* thing; they are an *all-the-time* thing.

Dr. Gilbert has given us the recipe. Do a little bit a lot of the time. Do it when you don't feel like it and you are not at your best. When the conditions aren't great, put on a raincoat. Thanks, Mr. D'Amato.

FROM THE SUCCESS HOTLINE ARCHIVES . . .

Tomorrow Begins Today

Dr. Rob: Four of the most powerful words in the English language are: *"on a daily basis."* When you can say, "I'm doing it *on a daily basis*," your "it" is bound to be successful—whether your "it" is dieting or studying or working out or reading or just about anything. Anyone can do it once or once in a while. The test is: Can you keep on doing it *on a daily basis*? It's been said that it takes twenty-one to twenty-eight days to form a habit. Once you do something *on a daily basis* for more than three weeks—it's a habit!

Whatever you do today, you'll do more of it tomorrow. Habits start out as thin, weak threads and end up as thick, strong cables. Aristotle said, "We are what we repeatedly do." So, today, start doing it . . . *on a daily basis.*

~Perfection is not attainable. But if we chase perfection, we can catch excellence.~

~Vince Lombardi~

■ ■ ■

START: IT IS THE START THAT STOPS MOST PEOPLE

T*he last excerpt. Wow!* You did it. Thank you for reading. I hope you feel energized and motivated. I certainly do while writing this. Enjoy!

My wife gets mad at me when I say something that is ***just that simple,*** so don't get mad at me! But really, just start. **Start**—not an acronym or formula—just a mindset to get moving, and get started.

What is that thing? What is that project? What is that routine that you want to follow? You just have to start. Put it on the calendar, and just start. Is it losing weight? Is it doing a TED talk? Is it applying for that job or starting that new relationship?

Whatever it is, just start. Dr. Gilbert has shared many times on the Hotline that it's the start that stops most people—and that includes me writing this book. I had a lot of irons in the fire while starting this and writing this, but I just started. I wrote a little bit each day and a different chapter when I could, but *starting* was the biggest hurdle. Start, build momentum, and keep rolling.

There is a story about two people who needed to cross a large lake. Both began building their rafts, constructing them, and putting them together. The first person got the raft to where it was safe enough and good enough to begin their journey. It wasn't perfect, but it was safe and would not sink, and she began her journey across the lake.

The second person also started to build their raft. They continued to build, look at it, bring neighbors over to look at it, and continued tinkering with it. They waited for the perfect weather day. They did some more research about design. They made some changes. They tweaked it. Eventually, they set a date to launch the raft two years from now.

Which person are you? Are you ready to set sail? Obviously, we don't want to put you in danger by taking a raft that was not safe or ready—but don't lose the point of the story.

Yes, you might not be an expert. You might not be ready. Yes, you might feel unsure, and yes, you will definitely feel uncomfortable, but it's the start, so start whatever it is that you want to accomplish, and keep doing it.

Over the years and over the different books and writings, I've shared many stories of the first time that I did something or accomplished something. When I started out, I was so unsure and had no idea what I was doing, but after a while, I got comfortable and found my way. **Start.** You'll be happy you did!

FROM THE SUCCESS HOTLINE ARCHIVES . . .

Dr. Rob: Thoughts on Starting

"Well begun is half done."
~Aristotle, Greek philosopher

"The beginning is the most important part of the work."
~Plato, Greek philosopher

"You don't have to be great to start, but you have to start to be great."
~Joe Sabah, professional speaker

~Be extreme.~

~Dr. Rob Gilbert~

■ ■ ■

CONCLUSION

IT'S ABOUT OTHERS

Wow. *I can't believe it's done.* A book, a tribute, a dedication to the amazing Dr. Rob Gilbert. I hope you enjoyed it all. It was such an honor and a pleasure for me to be part of this book for Dr. Gilbert. Thank you to all our friends and contributors, most especially, Dr. Rob! Their stories and their connections to Dr. Gilbert really made the book very special.

He has helped many people, and hearing their stories over and over throughout the book has been truly inspiring. ***I want to do more, be more, influence more, and make the world a better place because of Dr. Gilbert.***

It's great to be able to do something for him. *It's about others.* This theme is evident throughout his messages on the Success Hotline and his seminars. Almost everything he has done in his professional life was helping others. He and his desire and dedication to help others are truly amazing.

It's about helping and uplifting others. It's about making others feel special. Thank you, Ed Agresta, for your excerpt on this topic.

It is about you being the best you can be to do a great job of helping and inspiring other people. Whether you are a teacher, a professor, a salesperson, a coach, a parent, a principal, or *whatever*: *It's about others.* Dr. Gilbert has made this abundantly clear.

And when you can fill your bucket consistently over and over and take care of yourself on the journey, you will do a better job helping serve others.

We want to continue Dr. Gilbert's legacy and message about inspiring and helping others by starting an endowed award in his honor at Montclair State University. There's a QR code in the image below that would allow you to donate and participate in Dr. Gilbert's award, or you can type this address into your internet browser: https://bit.ly/DrRobGilbertAward

The award will be given to a Montclair State University professor every year with the following message. A portion of the online sales of this book will go toward this award each year.

***The Robert Ellis Gilbert Endowed Award for Positive Impact in Teaching Fund**, established in spring 2025, to honor Dr. "Rob" Gilbert and his impact as an Associate Professor in the Department of Kinesiology at Montclair State University for the past 45 years. Dr. Gilbert teaches sports psychology in the Kinesiology Department, where he has inspired students, alumni, parents, colleagues, fans, and friends through his classroom teaching, books, and the "Success Hotline." Anyone can call his Success Hotline and listen to his three-minute outgoing motivational message, where he has never missed a single day in 33 years! As of May 2025, he has left more than 12,500 messages!*

The Robert Ellis Gilbert Endowed Award for Positive Impact in Teaching will be awarded annually in the spring to a current faculty member who has positively impacted the lives of his/her students and the Montclair State University community over a significant period of his/her teaching career. This award honors a member of the MSU faculty who excels at teaching, inspiring, and mentoring undergraduate and/or graduate students. The honoree must demonstrate lasting dedication to ideals of higher education at Montclair State University and the highest standard of excellence, inspiring academic rigor, engagement, and intellectual curiosity. This award is meant to acknowledge a faculty member who demonstrates exemplary commitment to their students, is known for their passion for teaching, and inspires students, colleagues, and friends in similar ways. This award will be used to support the University and its programs that assist students.

Please join the many individuals who have been inspired by Dr. Gilbert as a teacher or through his Success Hotline, and make a gift today!

Please consider donating. If you have any questions, please contact the Office of Annual Giving at Montclair State University at 973-655-4141 or giving@montclair.edu.

So, as we close our journey together, remember this. *It's about others.* As I look back on my life, I tried to push myself up the ladder of success, sometimes forcing my way. I asserted myself in many ways, trying to be successful and significant as a husband and Dad, in my school community, the officiating world, and elsewhere.

As *Father Time* has turned my clock to fifty years old for me this year in 2025, I think more about my future and my family. I have embraced Dr. Gilbert's message. *It truly is about others.* The more people I can help on their journey, the better off I will feel and be. Doc has said this in his messages. Yes, the messages are helping others, but they really helped him, too! A true win-win.

After reading this book, I hope you will become a lifetime Hotline caller or podcast listener as well and feel the need and the urge to help serve others. Please donate to the award that has been established in honor of Dr. Gilbert!!! Thank you!

It has been a true honor to put so many of Dr. Gilbert's favorite acronyms, formulas, and impactful stories of leadership into this book. My mind sprints, and my heart pounds as I continue to try to be the best I can be to help and inspire others on their journey—all because of Dr. Gilbert and his amazing Success Hotline. I am forever grateful to him and thank him for all he has done for me and so many others. I hope the book has done the same for you! *Onward and upward—surviving and thriving all the way!*

With gratitude and kindness,

Andrew Marotta

APPENDIX

THE "CAST" OF SUCCESS HOTLINE

Every Single Person Who Has Ever Been Mentioned on the Success Hotline

Corinne Ellis Gilbert

Dr. Terrie

Earl Nightingale & "The Strangest Secret"

The Entire Carbonaro Family from Cuero, TX

The Entire Hoffman Family from Austin, TX

Eric Butterworth

Napoleon Hill

Al Pacino

Fazio

Bill Sharman

Paul Babcock & Mick

Dr. Paul Hartunian

Matt DiMaio

Mr. D'Amato

Robert Kraft—"The Raven"

Lee Kemp, world champion

Mark Gechtberg, world champion

The Banach Brothers—world & Olympic champions

Pete Rose & Ty Cobb

Cy Young

Bogna Wawrzeniuk

Scott Lenz

Scott Cochrane

Scott Hamilton

Mark Glicini, world champion

Chad Smith

Tom Holland

Max Cohen

Dan "Bull" Walsh

The Great Ed Agresta

Emma Rose

Tessa Marotta

Rich Kennedy

JFK

Timothy Hyland

Mark Housel

Rick Saldan

Dr. Rossi

Tom Hopkins and "The Champion's Creed"

The Waitress & the Mailman

The Three Frogs

Brian Cain

Randy Jackson & "The Royal Season"

Ethan Miller

Coach Frank Johnson

Debra Angel

Mr. Andrew Marotta

Mr. Jove Stickel

Karin Arbarbinal, Professor John Kenneth Galbraith, and Sinclair Lewis

Michael Jackson

Ted Williams

Muhammad Ali

Gene Zannetti

President Abraham Lincoln

Andrew/Tennessee

The Murphy Sisters

Mike Tyson

Buster Douglas

President Bill Clinton

Brady Furst

Wilma Rudolph

Karoli Takacs

Dr. Melissa Sapio & MTE

Dan Gable, world & Olympic champion

Coach Dan Gable

Mark & Bonnie Gechtberg

Jerry Rice & "Fight through it."

Dr. Joseph Donnelly

Tom Donnelly, world champion

Matt from Bricktown

Jim from Ringwood, R.I.P.

Anne Alworth, R.I.P.

Bill Zerden, R.I.P.

Tom Mapother II

The World's Most Confident Fourth Grader

Dennis Rogers

Russell Jones

Bud Jeffries, R.I.P.

Tom Fleming

Coach Lou Holtz

The Blues Brothers

Cus D'Amato

Dr. Mark McLaughlin

Melissa Owen

Jesse Owens

Rich Ruffalo, world champion

Dr. Rob Ruffalo & Broccoli Rob

Wes from Atlanta

Jake Herbert, Olympian

Dr. Christina Lang

Coach Maria Nolan

Ed Ferraro
Ed & Glenn
Bobby Penotti
Sue Brooks
Vince Burke
Ken Carberry
Coach Mike Tully
Anita Langley, valedictorian
Teddy Atlas
Jim & Ramona
Philippe Petite
Crystal Carter
Philippe Blondin
Tony Conigliaro
Dr. Kroll
Walter Kroll
Holly & Woody
Greg & Vincent Ferry
Loren Foxx
Foxx from Michigan
Terry Fox
Dr. Ken Ravizza
Coach Herb Brooks
Coach Tully
Jared Kahmar
Senator Corey Booker
Dr. Delate
Charles Laughton
Mark Bove
Coach Perry from Nixa
Chad Smith from Zionsville
Darren Ventre
Kathy Murphy
The custodian at NASA
Emery & her mom
Coach Barr
Donene Taylor & Chester, world champions
Jerry Rice
Milt Campbell, Olympic champion
Coach Aaron McKelky
Omar
Kelly Walsh High School
Tom Boud
Bobby Witt, Jr.
Josh Jung
Nicole
Tiger Woods
Jack Nicklaus
The Williams sisters
Jackie Robinson
Alexander Karelin
Joe Conway
Mme. Lise Fattel
Lise & David

Dr. Melissa Rivers from Western NY

Scott & Eliza

Michael Baldwin

Larry Bird & Bobby Orr

The US Gold Bureau

Sunny Michael from California

Dr. James Maas

Jim & Ali Stroker

Coach Cliff

Jim Fixx

Tony Robbins

Les Brown

Harry Winston

Blake & Knox Utley

The Gambler

The Raven

Joe Salas, author

John Stephen Akhwari

The Waitress & the Mailman

The Reunited Couple

Jill Jeffrey

Chris D'Andrea

Karoli Takacs

Mr. YouTube

Jerry Lucas

Mr. D'Amatro

The "I wish I had a brother like that" kid

Coach Pat Summitt

Coach John Wooden & Pyramid of Success

Coach Vince Lombardi

Coach Doc Councilman—hurt-pain-agony

The EXTREME BAKERY

Milt Campbell

Charlie Smith

"The Boys in the Boat"

Robin Williams & *Dead Poets Society*

Bobby Czyz, world champion

Bill Buckner

Henry Ford

Henry Peterson

Ryan Lockne

Coach Knute Rockne

Zig Ziglar

Les Brown

Kenny Rogers & "The Gambler"

Bill Russell

Bob Richards & "The Heart of a Champion"

Larry Owens

Larry Bird & Magic Johnson

Kathy Murphy

Superman & Wonder Woman

Dr. Stephen Covey

Dr. Christina Marie

Linda Faller

Coach Eric Luster, world champion

Coach Will Bishop, world champion

Pete Gonzalez

Joe Girard & the Law of 250

Bill Parisi

Martin Rooney

Rich "The Human Crane" Sadiv

Dr. Carol Dweck & "Mindset"

Dr. Angela Duckworth & "Grit"

Bill & Charlie

Jack & Leo

Michael Spence

Gian Paul Gonzalez

Dr. Wayne Dyer

"The Mighty Atom"

Thomas Edison

Norman Cousins

Dr. Christine Lyons

Aaron Havens

Tic-Tac-Toe girl

Mike Piazza & 1,390

P.T. Barnum & Bailey

Morris Goodman "The Miracle Man"

I want to hear you listening!

Dr. George Sheehan

Dr. Carlson

Dr. Glasser & "Positive Addiction"

Professor/Coach John McCarthy

The Great Gama

Chucky Mullins

Jackie Robinson & Branch Rickey

The Pepperoni Pizza Guy

Oprah

Bruce

Yoda

Einstein

Doug Her

Dr. Edmund Jacobson

Dr. Herbert Benson

Dr. Hans Selye

Dr. Michael Howard

Bonnie Consolo

Jack LaLanne

Dr. M. Scott Peck

Sylvester Stallone & "Rocky"

Rocky Marciano

YOU!
Bill W.
Paul Harvey
B.K.S. Iyengar
Pattabhi Jois
Dr. William James & habit formation
Joseph Campbell
George Bolan
Joe McAuliffe, world champion
"Joshua in a Box"
Dr. Maurice Massey
Gerry Citro
Ray Napolitano
Dr. Sundt
Covert Bailey
Eda LaShan
Nicolo Paganini
Jaime Escalante & "Stand & Deliver"
Dr. Paul Dudley White's theory
Jacki Sorensen
Mrs. Fields Cookies
Dr. Maxwell Maltz & "Psychocybernetics"
Dr. David Viscott
Chesley "Sully" Sullenberger
Dale Carnegie
Grandma & the lemon
Winston Churchill
Roy G. Biv
Eddie from So Cal
Coach Burnside
Garth Brooks
Jocko Willink
Dan Hardwick
John Goddard
Jim Carrey
John Morris
John Maynard Keyes
Ray Kroc
Bunny Leavitt
Fred Smith & FedEx
Tim Gallwey
Jim Abbott
Chad Bentz
Coach Joe Newton
Dr. Miguel Hernandez
Ben Hogan—train whistle
Willie Stargel
George Gipp
Frank Bettger
Joe Paterno's Blue Line
Jodi Reicher
David from David & Goliath
Teacher & the sun
One-Armed Judo Champion

Franklin Jacobs
Dolly Parton
The Old Man with the Roses on Valentine's Day
President Reagan
Bruce Baumgartner
Mother Mouse
Anna's mother
George Gershwin
The Chicken and the Pig
Irv Furman
The young boy & the starfish
Tom Hanks
Dr. George Horn
Nicolo Paganini (1782–1840)
Russell Conwell & "Acres of Diamonds"
Joshua Bell
Shun Fujimoto
Lee Trevino
Florence Chadwick
Johnny's sixth-grade teacher
The mailman
The elderly carpenter
Ralph the penguin
Ben Hogan
Fritz Kriesler
Og Mandino
Christmas quilt story
Ropa
Coach Lou Little
Babe Ruth
Dr. Rhonda Ellison
Angelo Dundee
Tim from West Hartford
Bobby Fisher
Tom Brady & Mike Piazza
"The Queen's Gambit"
Whitney Houston
Arthur Palacas
Tom Stewart, R.I.P.
Jim Rohn
Steven Iverone (do not pronounce "e")
Billy Mills
Jim Rohn
Terry Wright, West Jordan, Utah
Rudy Ruettiger
Brandon Steiner
Tom Petty
Cheerleading coach from Navarro
Ashrita Furman
Professor John McCarthy
Mike Tyson & Buster Douglas
Buzz Aldrin

Lance Rentzel
Maisie DeVore
Billy Hawkins
Sandy Koufax & Norm Sherry
Coach Don Martone
The little boy and the starfish
Kevin Chick-lo-mani
Frank Somma
Ed Tseng
Billy Pinckney
Bloomfield Barber
Don Mattingley
Cowboy and the red-hot coals
St. Peter and billable hours
The Texas oil man and the swimming pool
The engineer and the cruise ship
Frank Sinatra & "High Hopes"
Paul Reddick
Dr. Hal Abraham
Mary Cavernero
Coach Ralph Cinque
Dr. Rob Conenello
Doug Cooney
David Cooper
Chris D'Andrea #27
David Segro
Brett Ashley Davis
Charlie Del Rosso
Dr. Donna Dennis
David DeNotaris
Nick DiDominico
Chris Doelle
Dr. Kemberley Eagles
Jordan Falcone, world champion
Bonnie Ferrari
Brian Jude Pietkowski
Ellen Levine
Dave Levine
Lucky
Marge Conroe
Ray Miller
Mark Monteyne
Eric Moss
Anthony Niebo, computer genius
Tyler Pazik
Jake Beitz
Frank Perelli
Gary Pritchard
Evan Ruggiero
Nick Serpico
Ed Smith
James Taylor

Jimmie Vaughan
Veronica
Michael Vickson
Tony Vlohalek
Geo
Wes in Atlanta & Katherine
Santa & Rudolph
Stan Musial
Lisa Sargese
Jay Mills
Russ Waterman
Tom Collins
Kevin Guzzo
Emily Grace
Milo of Croton
Joshua Swift
Bella Love
Dr. Tyler Ley ("I love concrete.")
Lynne Brum

▪ ▪ ▪

FROM THE SUCCESS HOTLINE ARCHIVES . . .

A Success Hotline Quiz: Complete the Following Sentences

"It's the start that . . ."

"It's not what you're going through, it's what you're . . ."

"The important thing . . ."

"Shoot for the moon—even if you miss . . ."

"You have all the ability; all you are lacking . . ."

"Life is not a talent game; it's a . . ."

"Success leaves . . ."

"Do more than . . ."

"Things work out best for those . . ."

"Are you willing to give up what you want . . ."

"*Act as if* it were . . ."

"Everything you need is already . . ."

"If you have a big enough reason *why*, you'll . . ."

"The best team never wins; the team that . . ."

"Winners lose more than . . ."

"Be comfortable . . ."

"Good, better, best . . ."

"It's better to do a little . . ."

"Show up early, . . ."

"There's no such thing as winning and losing—just . . ."

"The pain of discipline weighs . . ."

"Prepare the child . . ."

"Everyone has a plan until . . ."

"A setback is a setup . . ."

"Don't quit, . . ."

"It's not the end of the road—just . . ."

"Don't place a period where . . ."

FROM THE SUCCESS HOTLINE ARCHIVES . . .

The Answers to the Success Hotline Quiz

"It's the start that stops most people."

"It's not what you're going through, it's what you're going to."

"The important thing is to make the important thing the important thing."

"Shoot for the moon—even if you miss, you'll be one of the stars."

"You have all the ability; all you are lacking is the correct strategy."

"Life is not a talent game; it's a strategy game."

"Success leaves clues."

"Do more than expected."

"Things work out best for those who make the best of the way things work out."

"Are you willing to give up what you want now for what you want most?"

"*Act as if* it were impossible to fail."

"Everything you need is already inside you!"

"If you have a big enough reason *why*, you'll find and do the *how*."

"The best team never wins; the team that plays best always wins."

"Winners lose more than losers lose."

"Be comfortable being uncomfortable."

> *"Good, better, best,*
> *Never, ever rest,*
> *Until your good gets better,*
> *And your better gets best."*

"It's better to do a little a lot than a lot a little."

"Show up early—something good is bound to happen."

"There's no such thing as winning and losing—just winning and learning."

"The pain of discipline weighs ounces. The pain of regret weighs tons."

"Prepare the child for the road, not the road for the child."

"Everyone has a plan until they get punched in the face."—Mike Tyson

"A setback is a setup for a comeback."

"Don't quit, can't fail."

"It's not the end of the road, just a bend in the road."

"Don't place a period where God has placed a comma."

FROM THE SUCCESS HOTLINE ARCHIVES . . .

The 12 Greatest Success Hotline Quotes of All Time

1. "Anyone can count the number of seeds in an apple. *No one* can count the number of apples in a seed."
2. The ten most powerful two-letter words: "If it is to be—it is up to me."
3. "Shoot for the moon—even if you miss, you'll be one of the stars."
4. "It's the start that stops most people."
5. "Because of this, something good will happen."
6. "It's better to do a little a lot than a lot a little."
7. E + R = O (Event + Response = Outcome)
8. Actions change Attitudes. Motions change Emotions. Movements change Moods.
9. "You can change your life by altering your thoughts." ~Eric Butterworth
10. "Your thoughts determine what you want. Your actions determine what you'll get." ~Fazio
11. "Don't quit—can't fail!!"
12. "*Act as if* it were impossible to fail."

FROM THE SUCCESS HOTLINE ARCHIVES . . .

Every once in a while on the Success Hotline, Dr. Gilbert throws out some "brainteasers" or "lateral thinking puzzles." Here are the ten best . . .

1. Romeo and Juliet lie dead in a pool of water in a room. The only clue to their death is an open window and broken glass on the floor. How did they die?
2. A man rode into town on Friday. He stayed for three nights and then left on Friday. How come?
3. If you have only one match and you walked into a room where there was an oil burner, a kerosene lamp, and a wood-burning stove, which one would you light first?
4. How many animals of each sex did Moses take onto the ark?
5. A clerk in the butcher shop is 5'10" tall. What does he weigh?
6. Five pieces of coal, a carrot, and a scarf are lying on the lawn. Nobody put them on the lawn, but there is a perfectly logical reason why they should be there. What is it?
7. A woman gave birth to two sons, who were born at the same hour of the same day of the same year. But they were not twins. How could this be so?
8. How many two-cent stamps are there in a dozen?
9. Make one word from the following jumbled letters: "o r e n o d w"
10. What occurs once in a minute, twice in a moment, but not once in a thousand years?

Brainteasers: The Answer

1. Romeo and Juliet were goldfish.
2. The man's horse was named "Friday."
3. You would light the match first.
4. Zero. It was Noah who had the ark, not Moses.
5. He weighs meat.
6. They are remnants of a melted snowman.
7. They were not twins. They were triplets.
8. There are 12 in a dozen.
9. The one word is "one word"!
10. The letter "m."

EVERYTHING YOU NEED TO KNOW ABOUT LIFE IN JUST *FOUR* WORDS

This too shall pass.

Live and let live.

No pain, no gain.

The past is practice.

Win arguments—lose friends!

Nothing ventured, nothing gained.

Live. Breathe. Laugh. Love.

Bad news travels fast.

Nothing succeeds like success.

Thank you very much.

"I have a dream."

Don't worry. Be happy.

Don't drink and drive.

Eat less. Exercise more.

"Show me the money."

"Wax on. Wax off."

GOYA

Shortcuts always cause problems.

Who? What? When? Why?

"Put me in, Coach."

Give peace a chance.

In God we trust.

Bark less. Wag more.

First come, first served.

Better late than never.

Do more than expected.

Still waters run deep.

Love laughs at locksmiths.

Charity begins at home.

Nothing ventured, nothing gained.

Man proposes, God disposes.

Let sleeping dogs lie.

▪ ▪ ▪

So now you have finished the book. What will you do first? You can't do it all in one day. Pick two or three things you *like the most* in the book, and *just start.* Do them well, do them often, and do them repeatedly. When you get better at them, make them part of your routines, and then slowly add a few more. A thick cable starts out as a thin thread that is woven over and over. The same with your habits. You've got this! Thanks for reading. Keep surviving and thriving.

With gratitude,

Andrew Marotta

DID YOU ENJOY
THE MAGIC ACRONYMS, FORMULAS, & IMPACTFUL STORIES OF LEADERSHIP?

Continue your journey with Andrew's other influential books and resources for businesses, families, educators, sports teams, Dads, and leaders:

The Principal: Surviving & Thriving
H.A.T.S: Heartfelt Acts for Teachers, Students, and Staff
Tales from the Hardwood: Surviving and Thriving
The School Leader: Surviving & Thriving
The Partnership: Surviving & Thriving
Dads, Leaders, & Father Figures

Discover more of Andrew's work and keep growing as a leader.

Available on Amazon, Audible, and andrewmarotta.com for wholesale purchase & personalized books.

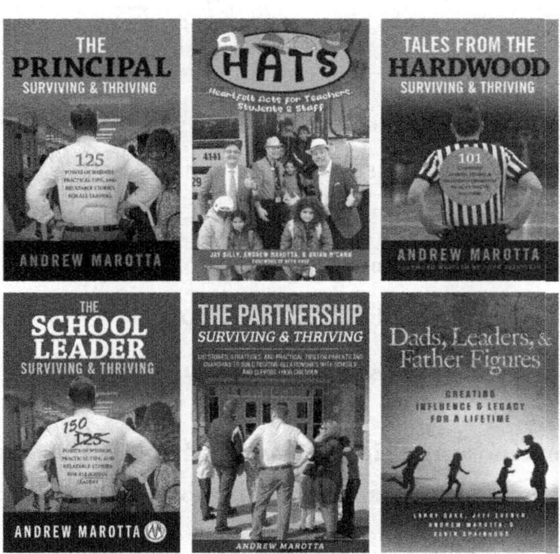

LEAD WITH PASSION, PURPOSE, AND COMMITMENT

PPC: Passion, Purpose, and Commitment is Andrew's signature **High-Impact Leadership Coaching** program designed to help leaders unlock their potential, elevate their performance, and make a lasting impact.

Passion • Purpose • Commitment

HIGH-PERFORMANCE LEADERSHIP COACHING WITH

Andrew Marotta

Through customized coaching sessions,
Andrew empowers leaders to:

Enrich their *Passions*

Elevate their *Purpose*

Live their *Commitment*

Learn more and sign up for *PPC* High Performance Leadership Coaching at andrewmarotta.com.

LEVEL UP YOUR LEADERSHIP ANYTIME, ANYWHERE

Looking for online, certified professional development? Want to be inspired but can't get away? Want a wide range of practical, reliable, and on-demand learning?

Andrew's ***Online, On-Demand Professional Learning Library*** through Responsive Learning gives you access to a wide range of practical, on-demand training for educators and leaders.

✓ **Flexible, self-paced courses**

✓ **Fresh ideas and proven strategies**

✓ **Professional growth at your fingertips**

Scan the QR code to start learning today!
Reach out to Andrew for wholesale pricing for your organization.

Or visit andrewmarotta.com to learn more.

BOOK ANDREW FOR YOUR NEXT EVENT

Are you ready to inspire your business, staff, students, or leadership community?

Andrew Marotta is an experienced engaging keynote speaker and leader who brings **contagious energy, impactful storytelling, and practical tools** to every stage—and your organization!
Popular Topics Include:

Be a Master Storyteller
Today's Significant Educator
People, Performance, & Pressure: Tales from the Hardwood
Be the One
Master Your Mornings
Today's Significant School Leader
Creating Schools that Kids are Excited to Attend
The Art of Communication to Build Meaningful Relationships
Above the Line Interactive Leadership Activity
The Uncommon Scenarios
Podcasting, Blogging, & Adding Deeper Value to Your School Community
Building Deeper Relationships to Create Better Student Outcomes
Be a Master Presenter: How to Make Incredible, Impactful, and Attention-Grabbing Presentations

Connect today to bring Andrew to your business, school, or organization!
Email Andrew at *andrewmarottallc@gmail.com.*
Learn more at *andrewmarotta.com*

Follow Andrew on all socials for daily inspiration and resources:
@marottaandrew on Instagram,
Andrew Marotta on FaceBook
@andrewmarotta21 on X.
Subscribe to Andrew's YouTube channel: AndrewMarotta5421

Made in the USA
Coppell, TX
30 December 2025